# Freedom to Fly

## 101 Activities for
## Building Self-Worth

# Freedom to Fly

## 101 Activities for
## Building Self-Worth

by Chris Brewer

Zephyr
Press

Tucson, Arizona

Freedom to Fly
101 Activities for Building Self-Worth

Grades 4–8

1993 by Zephyr Press
Printed in the United States of America

ISBN 0-913705-84-5

Editors: Stacey Lynn and Stacey Shropshire
Cover design: Nancy Taylor
Design and production: Nancy Taylor

Photographs were used with permission.
Gerald Askevold: pages 30, 121
Ellen Boyd: page 63
Joel Brown: pages 1, 110, 186, 188, 206
Tony Budessa: pages 6, 67, 170, 214
Karen Nichols: pages v, 136
Tim Robison: page 16
Sal Skog: page 76, 231

Cover photographs, clockwise from upper left: Tony Budessa,
Gerald Askevold, Joel Brown, and Karen Nichols.

Zephyr Press
P.O. Box 66006
Tucson, Arizona 85728-6006

Library of Congress Cataloging-in-Publication Data

Brewer, Chris, 1953–
     Freedom to fly : 101 activities for building self-worth / Chris
   Brewer.
       p.    cm.
   Includes bibliographical references (p. ).
   ISBN 0-913705-84-5
   1. Self-esteem in children. 2. Activity program in education.
   I. Title.
   BF723.S3B74 1994
   370.15'—dc20                                        93-30309

*Freedom to Fly* is dedicated with love to the spirit of Jeanne Hamilton, who showed me (and everyone she knew) the art of bringing out each person's self-worth and creativity.

*And what do we teach our children in school? We teach them that two and two make four, and that Paris is the capital of France. When will we also teach them what they are? We should say to each of them: Do you know what you are? You are a marvel! You are unique. In all of the world there is no other child exactly like you. In the millions of years that have passed there has never been another child like you. . . . You may become a Shakespeare, a Michelangelo, a Beethoven. You have the capacity for anything. Yes, you are a marvel.*

—Pablo Casals

# Contents

# Acknowledgments

I offer my appreciation, with great respect, to the many people whose work, experiences, and perspectives are shared in this book. Most important, I give a special thank you to the educators, parents, and administrators who read this book with the intention of giving children the freedom to fly.

The following photographers contributed their work: Gerald Askevold, Ellen Boyd, Joel Brown, Tony Budessa, Karen Nichols, Tom Robison, and Sal Skog. A special thank you is due Tricia King for supplying me with much of the following artists' work: Chris Atkinson, Whitney Baldwin, Jenny Bissell, David Brewer, May Brewer, Stacey Brown, Matt Butterfield, Michaela Christensen, Mae Clark, Sara Cook, Emily Cummings, Jason Curtis, Lindsey Dombroski, Bobbie Jacobsen, Tricia King, Clinton Lentz, Alicia Leukume, April Moore, Shana Moore, Travis Ober, Brandi Owen, Amanda Owens, Alicia Reiner, Carson Ring, Jason Robinson, Devin Schmit, Allison Tuszynski, Aimee Van Antwerp, William Wildanger, and Sheena Wolfe.

# Introduction

Identity
Connections

Communication
Listening and
expressing

The Journey
Life processes, experiences,
and visions

Harmony
The
environment

## Spreading Our Wings!

Self-worth is the backbone of the human being. A sense of worthiness
and trust in oneself provides the will to survive, the desire to create, the
ability to learn, and the courage to reach out and connect with another
human being. Without the physical backbone, there is no support for
the physical human structure. Without a backbone of worthiness, there
is no support for the life energy that is the basis for mental, emotional,
and spiritual human structure.

The building of self-worth goes back to basics—to the foremost human need to trust in one's ability to survive the knowns and unknowns of the world. Humans reach their basic goal—to love and be loved—when we believe that we are worthy and capable of communicating with and relating emotionally to others.

The greatest skill we can help our children develop is the ability to understand themselves and to relate to other living beings, communities, and the natural world with a deep sense of wonder for life. Without such relationships we are truly alone—adrift without meaning in what may seem to be an unkind world.

Relationships are two-way streets—they require not only that we reach out but that we open ourselves to receive from others. Giving and receiving form the basis of any relationship, whether it is sharing with a friend or enjoying a sunset and expressing our wonder and appreciation. The ability to give and receive equally is described in scientific terms as the development of an "open" system. In an open system, energy flows in a balanced exchange throughout. This balance of energy flow keeps the system strong, healthy, whole, and alive. An open system of relationships offers us support, opportunities for growth, and a chance to feel a part of a greater whole.

*Freedom to Fly* provides expressive ways to develop connections and relationships with others through activities that stimulate the senses and encourage creativity. Creation is our work and play—it is life itself. Every day we create the shape of our lives through actions, products, and relationships. We create everything from the health of our bodies to the nature of our home and belongings, expressions of art, our lifestyle, and methods of being with others. When we create, we make visible a part of who we are. It is our way of showing that we are in relationship with the world and that we participate in life. The belief that we are valuable, worthy people gives us the trust to create freely.

*Freedom to Fly* is a resource book of activities designed to develop important aspects of our selves, integrate relationship skills in curriculum materials, and help define our roles in nature, in community, and in the universe. This book does not address the intelligences of self-worth, the inter- and intrapersonal intelligences, through linguistic and logic skills. There are bountiful materials that do so. Instead, this book provides "active"-ities that develop trust in the self and the world through experiences that include but go beyond words.

Many people and organizations have recognized the importance of self-worth. A wide range of information is available on the subject. Through my years of classroom experiences, extensive research, and reading, and with the assistance of friends and coworkers, the structure for *Freedom to Fly* emerged. This philosophy of building self-worth is a model that reflects natural principles. Process, rather than product, is a primary focus of *Freedom to Fly*. The development of a product does not always ensure an understanding of the process involved, but by teaching the process we give students the ability to function independently, and more important, we give them the skills they need for cooperative interdependence.

The self-worth building cycle of this model is made up of interdependent parts that form a holistic approach to self-worth. Although the format of this book implies a step-by-step process, you can start at any place within the cycle and, by moving through all parts, gain insights and knowledge that improve self-concept. You will create a spiral of growth by repeating the cycle.

In this spiral of growth a person gains a sense of identity through repeated connections with the self: body, emotions, personal rhythms, family, ancestors, and nature. Participants experience communication as a dance between listening and expressing that develops a balance of cooperating, interrelating, and problem solving. They begin to understand the journey of life, which makes them aware of life processes, of the dynamic experience of life's offerings, and of a vision of the future through goals, dreams, and inspiration. With an understanding of the natural flow and rhythms of life, students can create an inner environment of harmony that enhances their relationships with the self, with others, and with nature. This harmony and a belief in their worth allows students to gain deeper personal understanding and spiral ever higher and further toward freedom to fly.

# CHAPTER ONE

# Reaching In: Identity Connections

*We all need to experience the freedom and joy of our own creative movement.*

*It makes no difference what age, size, sex, or what condition our bodies are in.*

*The feelings are the same in all of us.*

*We need to create, to express and be nourished as we learn from experiences which connect to our deepest selves.*

*There is no one who can be and dance like any other.*

*We all have our own genius when we allow it to emerge:*

*To be ourselves and to create;*

*To again capture the feeling of the child within us, along with our adult understanding;*

*And to allow that child to feel full freedom and expression.*

*We give this special gift of ourselves to our children:*

*We appreciate their individual beauty and create an environment and goals for them,*

*So that they can direct their natural high energy for constructive and fulfilling lives.*

—Teresa Benzwie
*A Moving Experience*

**S** ensing

**E** xpressing

**L** earning

**F** orming

Who am I? WHO am I? Who AM I? The age-old question echoes through the mind of each person. Every individual's self-worth is built upon the answers to this question, for it is these answers that give us meaning in life.

Understanding one's self begins with a personal exploration of body, mind, spirit, and emotions. As each person Senses-Expresses-Learns-Forms, he or she gains an appreciation of the nature of the SELF. The realization of self is also a recognition that identity comes from connections to the world around us. We answer the question "Who am I?" through our relationships with communities of people in the past, in the present, and in the future. We answer "Who am I?" by understanding our connections with nature and realizing our role in the life around us.

We cannot value something if we do not understand the meaning it holds. Each person must find his or her own answer to the Who am I? question in order to find individual value. As teachers, however, we can give students the opportunity to experience various aspects of SELF and give students support in developing their identity. Students' self-worth will grow as they understand more about themselves and appreciate their bonds to life.

The following Sensing-Expressing-Learning-Forming experiences will help students create and strengthen their identity bonds.

# The Body Connection

Shana Moore

When we look at ourselves or one another, the first clue we have to identity is often in the shape and structure of the body. Sometimes we place a great deal of importance on how our bodies look. Appreciating the differences between bodies without judgment and recognizing the role our bodies play as vehicles for living is an important part of learning to value ourselves and others.

The body is the machine that allows us to live, create, and communicate. Through our bodies we touch, feel, and manipulate the world around us. We express ourselves through body movements, stance, and actions. Our caring communication is often in the language of touch. The comfort and bonding that come through a caring touch can be a strong form of reassurance and acceptance.

Everyone's body has an intelligence of its own. An intimate connection with our bodies is important to gain confidence to move freely in the world. While some people move and work with their bodies easily, others find their bodies to be awkward and uncomfortable vehicles. By exploring how our bodies feel and move, we gain an appreciation of our abilities and limitations in the physical world.

The following activities are experiences in moving, feeling, seeing, and touching.

# 1 Facing Each Other

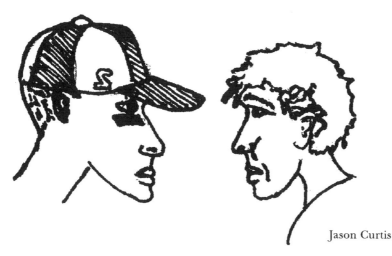

Jason Curtis

Our faces are the windows from our inner worlds to the outer world; the face is the body part that represents us most. In our language we often use the word *face* to represent who we are. We are careful not to "lose face," but strive to "save face" instead. We say that one has to "face the music," and if we are having difficulty in a relationship we say that we can "hardly face" the other person.

When we look at a person's face we soon become aware of the feelings that are on the other side of the "window." The mouth, forehead, eyebrows, and other facial features tell the emotional story. Faces are a focus of identity, and each face is as unique as each set of fingerprints. Faces also tell a cultural story and the history of each person's lineage. We can see the shape of a nose or the curve of a chin that has been replicated for generations.

In this activity, students face each other as unique individuals by taking the time to observe and learn from faces.

## Activity

Discuss with students how faces help define our identities through individuality, cultural representation, and family traits. Then ask students to look into mirrors and notice their unique facial features. Next, have students write a paragraph describing their facial features, and tell them not to put their names on the descriptions.

Collect the papers and give each student another student's description. Then have all the students sit in a circle and give them about five minutes—with no talking—to look at each other's faces (giggles are sometimes hard to avoid).

When the five minutes are up, let the students know it is time to "face up" to their descriptions. Have each student read the facial description you gave him or her and say who he or she thinks owns the face. Then give students five minutes to talk with each other until they find the owners of their facial descriptions.

Instead of handing out the descriptions, you may choose instead to number the descriptions and display them on a bulletin board. Give students a day or two to write down who they think each facial description describes.

# Flying Further

The following are related activities that you can use in biology, social studies, language arts, and visual arts.

* ★ Ask students to find partners and sit so they are facing one another. One of the partners displays an emotion using only facial expressions. The other partner becomes a "mirror" and reflects the expressions. For a more dynamic experience, ask students to express an emotion that is reflected in music you play in the background.

* ★ Discuss the science of genetics and how physical traits are passed through generations. Ask students to bring in photographs of their relatives and ancestors. Have students share their photos with partners and see if the partners can identify facial features that have been genetically maintained in various family members.

* ★ Take this opportunity to study facial anatomy.

* ★ Have the class explore facial characteristics of various peoples using photographs from magazines or social studies textbooks. Make a list of the characteristics of different ethnic groups' facial features. Display pictures of faces on a bulletin board and see if students can guess the ethnic heritage of the different people in the pictures.

* ★ Make face collages using pictures cut out of magazines. Have students write short poems or haikus about faces and glue their works on the collage. Display the collages in a "Gallery of Faces."

* ★ See how many sayings, metaphors, and puns about faces students can find. Make a list and post it.

★ Have students write a short character sketch of an imaginary or real person. The sketch should use facial descriptions to convey the character's identity.

Following are ways to explore faces developed by Teresa Benzwie (1988):

★ Play relaxation music quietly in the background and ask students to close their eyes and listen. When the students appear relaxed, ask them to explore their own facial features gently with their hands. Give them such directions as "Feel how long your nose is." "Feel how high your forehead is." "Feel your hairline and explore the texture of your hair." "Find your cheekbones." "What parts of your face are hard? What parts are smooth? What parts are soft, or rough, or straight, or curved?" You can experiment with different emotions by asking students to make angry faces and feel the shape of anger on their faces. Explore happiness, sadness, fear, disappointment, or other emotions in the same manner.

★ Play relaxation music and ask students to sit with a partner. Have them take turns exploring each other's face and head with their eyes closed. Ask that they be completely quiet and very gentle. When they are through, ask them to open their eyes and share how it felt to explore others' faces and to have their own faces explored. How are their faces different? How are they the same?

# 2 "Wanted for" Mug Shots

Carson Ring

This activity gives students a pat on the back for the things they do well and gives each child a chance to be the center of attention.

## Activity

Make "Wanted" posters for your students that have written descriptions of their faces but no pictures, or use a computer graphic of a bandit just for fun. Next, make up positive "wanted for" characteristics that fit each student's personality. Examples include "wanted for always smiling" or "wanted for helping others often." Put up one poster each week and give the students the week to guess who the person on the wanted poster is. Students will enjoy taking their posters home.

# 3 Mind Mapping the Body

A mind map is a revolutionary technique for brainstorming, organizing thoughts, and enhancing creative thinking. Students can use this simple technique to take notes or to create visual outlines of lectures or reading assignments. A mind map uses words and picture symbols to convey information in a nonlinear fashion. Children too young to write words can mind map using only symbols and pictures. The use of images and visual associations has been proven to enhance memory. Your students can use this helpful tool in any subject area. (For an example, see p. 167. For more information, see *Mapping Inner Space* by Nancy Margulies, Zephyr Press, 1991.)

In this activity, students use mind mapping to heighten their awareness of their bodies and to give them insight into how they feel about their bodies. This opportunity helps students appreciate and accept the differences and similarities among them.

## Activity

Tell students they are going to make mind maps that describe their bodies. In the center of a large sheet of paper, each student draws a circle. The circle should be small so that there is room to write around it. Inside the circle, students will write their names or draw symbols that express who they are.

Next, brainstorm with your students key parts of bodies and words about bodies (hair, eyes, legs, arms, weight, height, size, shape, and so on). Write these words on the board as students share them. Ask students to think about the colors, shapes, textures, abilities, and ways they use their bodies.

Let students create mind maps about their bodies. Post the maps on a bulletin board or make an art gallery in the hall.

> What lies behind us and what lies before us are tiny matters compared to what lies within us.
>
> —Ralph Waldo Emerson

# 4 | Moving Shapes

I have often told my children that the bodies they have are the only ones they will ever be "issued," so it is important that they take care of them. It is also important to help students develop a strong bodily intelligence, or ability to move and use their bodies, because their knowledge of their bodies will dictate their ability to participate in many activities.

We all use our bodies more freely and comfortably when we have had the opportunity to explore openly a broad range of movements. This activity allows students to explore a variety of body movements and teaches the body how to imitate what the eyes see others doing.

## Activity

Ask students to stand in a circle with enough space around them to move freely without bumping into one another. Have a volunteer stand in the center of the circle. Next, play a selection of music and ask the person in the center to make up a movement that reflects the sounds of the music and that uses only arms. The students standing in the circle imitate the leader's movement until you say stop.

Then ask the leader to name a body part and select a person from the circle to come into the center. This person becomes the new leader and creates a new movement with the body part the leader suggested. Students in the circle imitate the movement. Repeat the activity until each student has had a chance to lead.

## Flying Further

The following are related activities that you can use in geometry, numbers, and letters.

★ Have the leader make different geometry shapes (square, rectangle, triangle, line, and so on) with his or her body for the group to imitate.
★ Ask the leader to lead the group in imitating an animal movement. Add animal sounds for fun.
★ Help students learn letters and numbers by having the leader form a letter or number shape with body parts or with the whole body.

# 5 Growing Movements

Here is another opportunity for students to build body intelligence and identity. This activity can get students moving, so it also works well for getting out wiggles, releasing stress, and refreshing the mind and body before refocusing on quiet work.

## Activity

Play movement music. Ask students to form lines, shoulder to shoulder, with four or five students in a line. The person at the left end of the line begins by making a very small movement with any part of his or her body. The student next to the leader imitates the movement as closely as possible, but makes the movement slightly bigger. The next student imitates the movement, making it even larger. Each student down the line repeats the movement until the last person is making the movement as big as possible. The entire line continues to make the movements until all students in the line are moving. Students then select a new leader and repeat the process with a new movement.

## Flying Further

The following are related activities that you can use in math, letters, numbers, grammar, and spelling.

★ Have students draw a letter or a number in the air. To add interest, students can try to draw the shape with a body part other than their fingers: try elbows, knees, one foot, the left hip, the head, or the tongue!
★ Have students draw numbers, do problems, or spell words in the air in the same manner.

> A child's life is like a piece of paper on which every passerby leaves a mark.
> —Chinese proverb

# **6** Living Sculptures

Sculpting is another activity that you can use to help students build their self-esteem. The ability to think and act out various roles and behaviors can be a turning point in students' believing that they can be and do many things.

> Sculpting can inspire the imagination. Make the impossible possible. What can I be? Where can I go? What is possible for me? What if I were a ballerina, brave, strong. I would like to feel beautiful, handsome, gentle and loving, successful. Sculpting helps to dramatize situations. I want to sculpt a perfect family for myself, how I feel, my favorite environment. . . . Sculpting stimulates children's imaginations and frees them to role play body movements.

> —Teresa Benzwie

# Activity

Students will follow your directions, moving until you say *"Freeze."* The students stop immediately and hold their poses until you give the next directions. Play music to help students move more freely. You may begin with a warm-up, telling students to walk slowly and softly; to walk backward; to walk sideways; to skip high; to make rounded movements; to move very stiffly; to move as if they were made of sticks.

Once the students are warmed up, you can have them move as they would expect people in different situations to move. For example, tell students to move as if they were ballerinas, as if they were scuba divers under water, as if they were astronauts on the moon, as if they were important executives, as if they were nervous fathers awaiting the birth of their children, as if they were store clerks arranging merchandise, as if they were people they would like to be.

Once you have told students to freeze, ask a few of them who they are. You can use all types and combinations of movements at various speeds. While students are frozen into poses, have them look at each other's "sculptures."

You might also try including some sculpting that reflects difficult life situations. Ask students to move as if they were on crutches, as if they were frustrated parents, as if they were in wheelchairs, as if they were tired but can't sleep, and as if they were very sad people.

# Flying Further

The following are related activities that you can use in history, science, and social studies.

★ Ask students to move as if they were someone they are studying in their history lessons: an explorer paddling up the Missouri River, Paul Revere on his famous ride, a miner panning for gold, a leader for the women's suffrage movement. You can also divide the class into three or four groups, give them each a secret person from their history studies to mime, and see if the other groups can guess who it is.

★ Lead students through movements that reflect various weather or seasonal patterns (a thundercloud, lightning, fog), different forms of matter (gas, liquid, solid), or geological phenomena (an erupting volcano, an earthquake, a landslide).

★ Have students create human sculptures to imitate the following: various forms of transportation (cars, boats, bicycles, trains, planes), various occupations (scientists, doctors, sailors, musicians, miners), various cultural activities.

# The Emotional Body

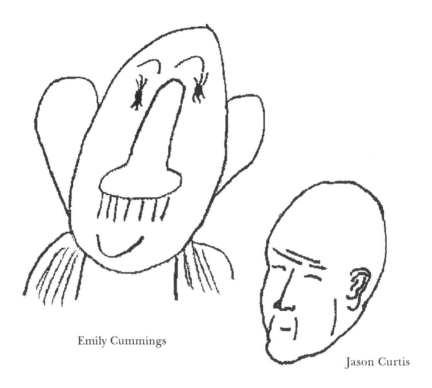

Emily Cummings

Jason Curtis

We don't see emotions in the same way we see physical objects, but emotions do govern many of our actions and behaviors. In many ways, feeling is a form of thinking. Studies of memory have shown that we remember information that has an emotional content much more easily than we remember information that is not attached to feelings. The ability to sense and express oneself in subtle emotional ways has been correlated with abilities to perceive subtleties in critical thinking. We can gain a lot of information about how we think by understanding how we feel.

As we grow and develop, we learn about the logical thinking capabilities of our brains and the potential and limits of our physical bodies. We identify strongly with our bodies and thoughts. Learning to recognize who we are emotionally and how we want others to identify us in regard to our emotional makeup is very important in forming an identity. Whatever we do—whether at work, at home, or at play—we are involved in human relationships, and our emotions play a key role in our interactions. If we have an understanding of our emotional bodies, we can use our emotions as tools in relationships in much the same way we use our minds as tools in learning.

We each have patterns of emotional ups and downs and can learn to predict our emotional behavior as well as to recognize patterns in others. The science of chronobiology, the study of biological rhythms, has determined that our emotional moods follow patterns that flow in a variety of time lines: daily, weekly, monthly, even yearly. Some patterns are universal. The grieving process, for example, follows an established, recognizable cycle.

Our skills for thinking and living develop through imitation, experimentation, and practice. Today there are many workshops, books, and programs on handling stress, on marriage and relationship issues, and on positive communication within the workplace. Most of these are after-the-fact lessons to repair problems. Teaching our children about their emotional bodies early in life can put them far ahead in the development of their living skills.

To learn about emotions students need the opportunity to experience, express, and evaluate their feelings. While some children may have rich emotional experiences at home, others may suffer from paradigms in which emotional expression is taboo, where "boys don't cry," where anger and rage prevail, or where fear is not allowed. These children especially need a place to gather a wide repertoire of emotional experiences. Some children may be so stuck in one particular emotion (often fear or anger) that they are incapable of functioning within the classroom until they have an opportunity to get in touch with their emotions.

The following activities provide doorways to emotional expression. Other sections of the book will expand these concepts by using emotions as tools in communication and learning. I include opportunities to explore the emotions involved in life processes and experiences throughout the book.

# 7 Sound Emotions

The voice has a great deal of emotional information. Sometimes we can understand more about people's emotional state if we listen to the emotional tone behind their words rather than the actual words. The voice quality often reflects feelings that the words are not expressing.

By sharpening our listening skills we can enhance our awareness of the cues in the voice and perceive others' emotions. When we explore the voice as a mode of expression we may access emotional states we have never allowed ourselves to acknowledge. When we use our voices in new ways we expand our range of feelings.

Don Campbell and I have experimented with the voice, sound, and emotions at Don's Institute for Music, Health, and Education. We enjoyed and learned from our experiments. Following is one of my favorite activities.

## Activity

Have your students imagine that the entire class has been magically transported to a new world where only long vowel sounds (aaaaa, eeeee, iiiii, ooooo, uuuuu) are spoken. Communication results from the feeling within the voice. Ask students to share happiness with each other by repeating, with a happy inflection, aaaaa, then eeeee, then iiiii, ooooo, and uuuuu after you. Be sure you draw out the sound enough to express a feeling of happiness in the emotional tone.

Repeat the vowel series, but this time have the students do it with you, and let the sounds reflect fear. Continue to repeat the series, each time with a different emotion: anger, sadness, excitement, pride, discouragement, wonder. As you do the activity, ask students to look for changes in their bodies with each new emotion. Do their postures change as they express the different emotions? Do their facial expressions change?

Now have students repeat the vowel series again but change emotions with each vowel, for example, a happy aaaaa followed by a sad eeeee, an angry iiiii, an excited ooooo, and a fearful uuuuu. Experiment with various combinations of vowels and emotions. Students can have emotional conversations, using only long vowels, with partners. You can also ask a student to lead the class in voicing these sound emotions.

# 8 Emotional Charades

David Brewer

Here's another sound and emotions activity I used to do as a music teacher. I called it "emotional charades." Students from kindergarten through eighth grade often requested this activity!

## Activity

Have students form groups of two or three. Say to them,

> *You are going to create sounds and movements that describe a scene I will give you. Use actions and nonword sounds to act out your charade. You may not use recognizable words in your scene, but you may use your voice, your body, or objects you find in the classroom to make sounds. Be sure to keep the topic of your scene a secret, and the other students will have to guess what your scene is. You will have five minutes to create your emotional charade.*

My younger students often became so involved in trying to decide what nonword sounds to make that they would forget to do the actions. I found that these students could focus on their emotions and actions better if I told them that they could only repeat the alphabet or numbers one through ten.

Next, give each group a scene to portray. You can use suggestions from the list below or make up your own.

Excited children at a circus

Waking up in the morning feeling tired

The meeting of two friends who begin visiting and then get into an argument

A parent angrily scolding her apologetic child for breaking something

A child consoling her sad friend

Two friends walking up to a door that has something scary behind it

An anxious parent waiting for a child, who is late, to return home

A bored student listening to a lecture

Have the groups find places in the room or in the hall where they can work on their sound scenes. Move from group to group to assist with ideas. After five minutes, have the groups come together to present their emotional charades and to have other students guess what the charades are. Students may need to repeat their scene for the other students to guess what the scene portrays. Once students get the hang of the charades, they are often delighted to come up with their own ideas for scenes.

# Flying Further

The following are related activities that you can use in history, science, and language arts.

★ Give students suggestions for scenes from the current history lessons and have the class guess which historical event the students are portraying.

★ Have students depict science scenes: geologic formations (metamorphic rock, volcanoes), biological processes (cell division, photosynthesis, the water cycle), chemical structures and reactions (atomic structure, covalent bonding), general science (plant growth, water tension).

★ Give students descriptive words such as *vastness, peacefulness, chaos.* Ask students to find a way to depict the feeling of the word.

# The Many Faces of Emotion

David Brewer

This activity explores how people express emotions with their faces and bodies.

## Activity

Have students select emotions they would like to explore and ask them to look through magazines and books for cartoons, drawings, and photographs of people who are expressing those emotions. Have them cut out or make photocopies of the expressions. Ask students to examine the pictures carefully and notice what kinds of lines are used to create the facial expressions. What kinds of body positions reflect the emotions? Next, have students create their own drawings of people that express the emotions. Students can use the examples they found as guidelines.

When students have completed their drawings, ask them to write a paragraph that describes how they feel when they experience the emotions in the drawings. Attach the descriptions to the drawings and post them on a bulletin board.

# 10 Feeling Sculpture

Following is an activity based on body sculpting that explores how our bodies express emotions. It will help students become more aware of their feelings.

## Activity

Have students choose partners and take turns "sculpting" one another into a position that expresses an emotion. If the sculptors haven't told their "clay" what emotion they are sculpting, the completed "feeling sculptures" can say what emotion they feel in the sculpted position. Students can switch emotions and take turns sculpting these different feelings.

> It is my conviction that education without self-knowledge in depth is a process which, like education itself, is never complete. It is a point on a continuous and never-ending journey. It is always relative, never absolute. It is a process which must go on throughout life, if at all; and like the fight for external freedom, it demands eternal vigilance and continuous struggle.
>
> —Lawrence S. Kubie

# 11 Racing My Emotions

What kid doesn't love a race? Here's a race that requires students to express an emotion quickly, before they can get to the finish line. Emotional expressions seem to jump out of students, since they don't have time to think about the emotion but just feel and express it.

This activity is good for exploring a range of emotions. It's also great for releasing pent-up feelings, getting rid of stress, and having a few laughs. Even adults enjoy this one.

Make sure you hold this race where there is ample room for running and playing.

## Activity

Ask students to form equal-numbered teams of seven or eight students. Select a student from each team to be the emotion "dealer." The teams line up approximately 15 to 20 feet from a marked goal, and the dealer stands at the goal. The dealer's job is to hand out slips of paper you have prepared, each with an emotion written on it. For the most fun, provide a variety of emotions.

Now the race is on. At the word "Go!" the first student from each team runs to the team's goal, is given an emotion to express by the emotion dealer, turns around to face the team, and performs a sound and a movement that expresses the emotion. The student must make the sound and movement three times before he or she can run back to the team. The next player then runs to the goal, receives and performs his or her sound and movement three times, and runs back to the team.

This highly emotional race continues until each student has completed an emotional sound and movement. The fastest-feeling team wins, although in some ways everybody wins because everyone has a chance to let loose a little bit.

# 12 Lining Up Feelings

Alicia Leukume

This activity encourages self-expression in movement and drawing. Students will see how feelings can be portrayed by drawing lines in response to movements made by students expressing a particular emotion.

## Activity

You will need an open area with room to move freely, large sheets of unlined paper, and colored markers or pencils. Divide the class into two groups—one to move in a way that portrays a feeling and the other to illustrate the movements. Explain to one of the groups of students that they are the artists and the other students are the movers. Give the movers a movement idea from the list that follows. (The list is also included in the appendix so you can copy it more easily.) Distribute the pencils or markers and paper to the artists. Be sure not to let the artists know what movement idea you have given the movers.

Ask the movers to imagine the feeling of the idea. Use the examples, or your own examples, to help them get into the feel of the emotion. After a moment of imaging, tell the movers they can begin to move in a way that expresses the movement idea.

Next, ask the artists to make lines on their papers to reflect the way the movers are moving their bodies. Allow three minutes for the artists to draw.

Let the movers sit while the artists show their pictures. See if the artists can guess the movement idea. Do the artists' lines reflect the feelings? Now have the students switch roles and ask the artists to move while the movers draw to a new movement idea.

## Movement List

**ANGRY:** How would you feel if you overheard someone saying something untrue about you?

**JOYFUL:** How did you feel when you learned to ride your bicycle or reached some other goal?

**SAD:** How did you feel when a good friend moved away or a pet died?

**EXCITED:** How did you feel when you found out your family was going to do something special?

**SNEAKY:** How did you feel when you tried to steal a cookie when no one was looking?

**LONELY:** How do you feel when you are left alone and you don't want to be?

**PEACEFUL:** How do you feel when you are snuggled in bed at the end of a great day?

**SICK:** How do you feel when you have the sniffles or the flu?

**HEALTHY:** How do you feel when you have been eating foods that are good for you and you've had plenty of sleep?

# Flying Further

The following are related activities that you can use in language arts, science, and art.

★ Use language from literature for movement ideas: a leaf falling from a tree, a rabbit hopping, popcorn popping, a snake slithering, a bird flying, a top spinning, a robot moving abruptly.

★ Use movement ideas that reflect science concepts: the formation of sedimentary rock, magnetic attraction, weather patterns, the laws of motion, wave intensity.

★ Have students come up with their own movement ideas.

# 13 Switching Hats

Sarah Cook

This activity is based on Edward de Bono's communication model in *Six Thinking Hats* (1985). De Bono explains that there are various ways to approach an issue, and he uses the idea of putting on special hats to think in each of these ways. Sometimes we develop an affinity for handling all of our issues through only one perspective. There are times when we can benefit from looking at a problem in new ways.

You can have a lot of fun in the classroom with the hat metaphor. Once students have become accustomed to the system, they will adapt to the communication model readily.

## Activity

Share with your students de Bono's six different ways of addressing an issue and the related hat colors. Have students form six groups, then have each group make a hat so that you end up with a hat for each color. Discuss with students the times when each hat would offer the most appropriate perspective. When would it be inappropriate to put on a scientific hat or an emotional hat?

**Blue:** Cool, calm

**White:** Neutral, scientific

**Yellow:** Positive, bright, "sunshine"

**Red:** Emotional

**Black:** Critical, problem-finding, looking for negative aspects

**Green:** Creative, insightful, curious

You can use the hat technique in many ways in your classroom and with other groups. Following are some suggestions:

★ Make a poster that displays each colored hat and the appropriate thinking perspective. Hang it in the room where students can see it for reference.

★ Get a hat of each color. Put on the appropriate hat when you are dealing with an issue or even a classroom subject to let students know what perspective you are taking.

★ When you want students to use a specific perspective in their studies or with a class social issue, draw a picture on the board of a hat and fill it in with chalk of the appropriate color.

★ As an example of a way to use the hats in school studies, consider a historical event. Discuss with the students how the event could be viewed from the perspective of each of the hats. You can use the same technique for current events, a novel, or social studies.

You may want to read de Bono's *Six Action Shoes* (1991) for more ideas.

# Energy Cycles and Circles

In "Rhythms of Education"(1992), I noted that rhythm is a universal aspect of life. Scientific research has revealed that every element of nature—even the smallest life form—vibrates in a particular rhythm. Within our bodies pulse rhythms of breath, heartbeat, cycles of energy and attention, hunger and sleep—every aspect of our existence. Even though we may not be aware of the rhythms, they guide and direct our lives. Each person's physical, mental, and emotional rhythms are unique and fluctuate throughout the day in recognizable patterns. Once we understand the flow of our own rhythms, we can enhance our ability to communicate, learn, and live in harmony with the world around us. We can match our daily tasks with the energy we have.

I originally began exploring personal rhythms when I was a K–8 music teacher, long before I knew anything about mandala therapy, the use of circle drawing to reflect inner feelings, or chronobiology, the scientific study of biological rhythms and cycles. I happened on the concepts through an activity that was intended to deepen children's listening skills and to help them realize that we have auditory environments or "soundscapes," as Canadian composer Murray Schaefer calls them. A version of this activity is in chapter 2 in the section on listening.

In the soundscape activity I asked the students to close their eyes and listen carefully to the sounds around them. We would discuss the sounds we heard and then I would ask the students to think back to the morning and remember the sounds they heard as they moved from sleep to wakefulness. I asked them to draw the sounds of their "morning soundscape" to reflect what they normally heard in the morning and how they felt because of their morning auditory environment.

The students were to draw a large circle first and then, starting inside the circle, use only lines, shapes, and colors to express their feelings. Drawing within circles to reflect inner feelings is used in mandala (or circle) art therapy. Carl Jung and others have developed specific techniques for revealing the psychological significance of the colors and shapes that a person uses in this type of circle drawing. Jeanne Hamilton, artist and founder of the Creativity Center, and I had been using this type of drawing in our workshops and therapy work. We find that people gain personal insights from this kind of artwork, and most often we let them arrive at their own answers.

In my classes, when students had finished their soundscape drawings, we compared the drawings and then talked about and drew other soundscapes in our lives. We played with many soundscapes, focusing on everything from evening, school bus, and playground sounds to circus, barnyard, and traffic sounds.

After using this exercise with many children, I was astounded by how this simple activity about morning soundscapes could reveal so much information to both the students and me. For some children it was merely a reflection of pleasant family voices, busy kitchen sounds, and the beginning of another day. But for others there were immediate revelations of the tensions in students' lives that began with their first waking moment. I could also see that there were significant, visible differences between the drawings that accurately pinpointed students who were "morning" people, with high energy in the morning, and students who were "evening" people and didn't get their energy levels up until midday. I knew how differently the morning and evening children approached the school-day activities and how these differences in energy levels affected their success in learning.

Intrigued by the fact that our soundscape drawings were reflecting not only the students' auditory environments but also their energy levels and emotional states, I shared my findings with Jeanne. We began experimenting with "moodscapes" and "rhythmscapes" during workshops by having participants make morning, afternoon, and evening mandala drawings. With all three drawings, people could reflect on their physical, mental, and emotional energy flow throughout the day. Often people would see a recurring energy slump that caused problems, and they would find ways to work around their low energy levels. Sometimes people would discover an emotional tension that carried from one part of the day to another. They would be amazed at how they carried emotional baggage with them, and we could see them begin to think about how to release the emotional tension. When people were able to reflect on the rhythm and flow of their day with the benefit of having a visual "chart" of this flow, they could understand themselves better and take responsibility for creating a more optimal daily routine.

I now realize how much our personal rhythms affect our daily lives and our relationships. I have also witnessed how these rhythms affect our ability to function in the world and how they shape the image we hold of ourselves. Developing a sensitivity to internal rhythms should begin early in life. By allowing time in the classroom for students to determine their natural attention and energy patterns, you will be helping students learn to use personal rhythms effectively.

The energy rhythms activities attune students to their unique patterns of energy and attention and help them gain information about themselves that they will use for the rest of their lives. The activities include both intuitive, artistic methods of exploring energy rhythms and scientific modes of analyzing biological cycles. I have also included a few quick, easy methods to bring energy levels down or give them a boost. Students can use these methods when they feel a need to change their energy level, and teachers can initiate the methods as class activities when the overall classroom energy would benefit from a change.

# 14 Energy Cycle Circles

This activity allows students to get a visual picture of the rhythm of their daily activities and the flow of their energy levels. It is a good first step toward sensitizing students to their personal rhythms. You may want to do the Soundscapes activity (page 80) as an introduction to Energy Cycle Circles.

Two of my fifth-grade music students drew these pictures as representations of morning soundscapes. Joel described his morning soundscape as a gradual awakening with a slow increase of sound, and Michelle described her awakening soundscape as abrupt, involving considerable stress and outside stimulation.

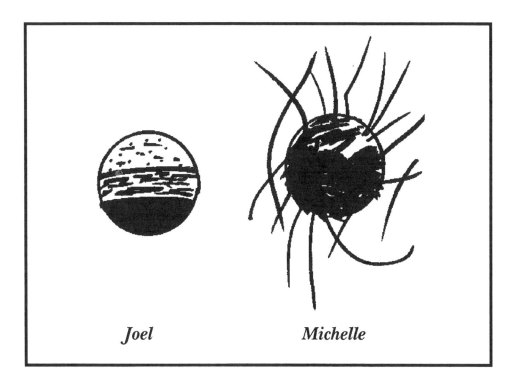

*Joel*                    *Michelle*

Michelle confided in me that she was awakened each morning by her stepmother, who yelled at her to get up. Michelle said she then yelled back at her stepmother, and a morning of arguments would begin. Michelle was very angry at school. The other students didn't really know what to do with her anger, and they mostly avoided her. Michelle used to spend a lot of her free time in my music room, where she could listen to music. She sang whenever she got a chance. I used to think she needed the sound just to block out the angry voices in her head. The year after she drew this picture, Michelle moved to another state to live with her mother and stepfather. I met her stepmother a couple of years later and found that she had been just as frustrated with Michelle as Michelle had been with her.

# Activity

Explain to students that we all have unique rhythms of energy highs and lows that repeat on a daily basis. These energy cycles affect how our bodies feel, how clearly we are able to think, and how we feel emotionally throughout the day. Let students know that this activity will help them understand how their personal energy flows throughout a day by giving them a way to draw their energy cycles. It often helps to show an example of energy cycle circles. You may want to draw circles similar to Joel's and Michelle's on the board and share their stories.

Next, ask students to close their eyes and remember how they felt in the morning as they were waking up. Ask them to remember their energy levels from the time they awoke until lunch. What are their main feelings? How does their energy change?

When students have the feelings set in their minds, ask them to draw three circles anywhere on a large sheet of paper. Drawing around the large end of a paper cup works well for making the shape. I never tell students where to draw the circles on the paper because they may place or connect the circles in a way that is important to the picture of their energy cycles.

Next, have students create an image in one of the circles using only lines, shapes, and colors to reflect the mental, physical, and emotional rhythms of their morning. Colored markers or oil pastels seem to work best for this activity. Give students five minutes to complete their morning energy circles. Then ask students to think about their energy levels from after lunch until dinnertime and to draw an afternoon cycle in the second circle. In the last circle, students make an energy cycle circle for evening, covering roughly the hours from dinner until bedtime.

When students have completed all three cycle circles, have them share their circles with partners, explaining how their energy fluctuates throughout the day. It's helpful for you to know about each child's energy patterns so you can help him or her work through low energy times and perhaps improve learning. You might go so far as to have a five-minute conference with each child and make notes on their energy patterns. You can post the energy cycle circles on a wall so everyone can see them; they are interesting to look at and help students understand one another better.

# Flying Further

You can use the circle drawing technique to provide an intuitive, artistic method of working with history, science, and music. Here are some ideas:

★ After reading a history lesson, ask students to draw circles using only lines, shapes, and colors to reflect the feelings of a specific historical event. Have students label their drawings and write a paragraph describing the significance of the historical incident. Have them include names, dates, and other specific facts in the description. If students do "history scapes" regularly, they can keep the scapes in a special notebook or folder. Students can share or trade their drawings and notes with a friend as a way of studying.

★ Ask students to draw circles that reflect the five Earth systems: lithosphere, biosphere, hydrosphere, heliosphere, and atmosphere. Students may want to use symbols in these drawings. Ask students to write a paragraph describing the essential aspects and cycling processes of each system next to their drawings. The sphere drawings may be displayed or used as study guides.

★ Ask students to listen to music from a specific era, music of a particular culture, or music emphasizing a particular instrument. As students listen, have them make circle drawings that reflect the musical sound. Label the drawings and display them in the classroom or use them as study guides for music class.

★ Ask students to be aware of their food intake. Have them make an energy cycle circle when they feel they have had a balanced breakfast and another one when they feel that their breakfast was not particularly balanced. Note the differences. You may want to do the same activity for sleep patterns, exercise, or other health issues.

# 15 Energy Charts

Body temperature coincides very closely to energy and attention cycles. Generally, higher body temperatures reflect higher attention and energy levels. Chronobiologists have determined peoples' energy patterns by charting temperature readings regularly throughout the day. Researcher Julian Biggers has conducted a number of energy level studies through temperature readings in educational settings and has found students very receptive to the experience. You can tie this activity into science and mathematics projects easily.

Students love studying their own chronobiology. Their energy cycle charts will also help you understand the patterns of students' attention. This activity is very analytic. To help students get in touch with their energy and attention patterns intuitively, you may want to have students do the Energy Cycle Circles activity first.

After students have charted their energy cycles, you may want to give students the flexibility to work within their optimal energy and attention periods by providing alternative times to work on subjects that demand intense concentration. One math teacher divided mathematics work into routine problem-solving practice and lecture time for learning new concepts. Then he scheduled two daily math periods, one in the morning and one in the afternoon. Students had the option to do the routine problem-solving during their lower energy times and save their high-attention peak time for concentrating on learning new concepts. Needless to say, students' math grades rose and the students were happier with their learning, which was definitely a boost to their self-esteem.

## Activity

Give each student a copy of the Temperature Cycle Chart and purchase a number of easy-to-read digital thermometers. Have students take their temperature every other hour during school hours and record the readings. You may even want to assign temperature readings as homework to have a picture of a full day of students' energy cycles.

After your students have recorded their temperatures for three or four days, a pattern should emerge. You can have students determine the average temperature for each hour as a mathematics exercise. With these figures, students can chart their own temperature variations and arrive at a scientific determination of their daily energy flow.

You may notice correlations between students' energy and temperature peaks and students' ability to concentrate. Students will benefit from taking a few minutes to note how they feel during their daily high and low peaks of temperature fluctuations. Keep the temperature charts for future reference.

# Temperature Cycle

| Temperature | 8 am | 9 am | 10 am | 11 am | Noon | 1 pm | 2 pm | 3 pm |
|---|---|---|---|---|---|---|---|---|
| 99.6 | | | | | | | | |
| 99 | | | | | | | | |
| 98.6 | | | | | | | | |
| 98 | | | | | | | | |
| 97.6 | | | | | | | | |
| 97 | | | | | | | | |

# Flying Further

The following are related activities that you can use in biology and health.

★ Explore the chronobiology of energy and attention rhythms more closely by researching fluctuations in brain-wave rhythms and body chemistry. Have the class find out the best times for various activities based on scientific research. (See Brewer and Campbell [1991] for information about optimal times for memory processing, rote learning, math calculations, physical activities, and other types of study.)

★ Study related biology topics as students learn about their daily rhythms: normal and abnormal body temperatures, sleep cycles, hormone functions, heartbeat and respiration rates, blood pressure levels. How do these vary during the day and what are the chronobiology cycles related to each of these systems?

★ Study other natural cycles: weather, lunar, geologic, historical, chemical. See what parallels you can draw between cycles in nature and human cycles. How do seasonal cycles, weather conditions, or holidays change our rhythms? Have the class do a project to research the effects of light, time of day, food, and exercise upon daily rhythms.

★ Study energy patterns in natural cycles. What is energy? What are characteristics of energy? How does it flow through a food chain? A car engine? How many forms of energy do we use for power sources for human consumption?

# 16 Sound Energy Infusions

May Brewer

These three activities will infuse a little more energy into tired bodies, rejuvenate overworked minds, and raise downtrodden spirits. They are especially useful for those low periods everyone has in the energy cycle. Let students know that they can do any of these when they feel their energy level drop. I've added goal-building and problem-solving suggestions to each of the activities to make them more potent for maintaining a positive self-image.

## Activities

### Aaaaah Break

Ask students to stand and release a long, loud sigh. Have students breathe deeply and sigh again, this time making the sound "aaaaah" as they sigh. Suggest that students imagine releasing negative feelings as they exhale and bringing in positive thoughts as they inhale. Make the sighs louder and longer until everyone has sighed away all their tired energy and negative feelings!

### Three Cheers for Life!

Take a few seconds to have everyone join in an invigorating Hip! Hip! Hooray! to celebrate the end of a test, to honor an important class event, to show appreciation for a student's special accomplishment, to acknowledge how good everyone is at learning, to rejoice that the sun is out or that the rain is nurturing the plants, or just to celebrate life itself!

### The Siren Rescue Machine

All emergency vehicles have sirens to warn other drivers of their approach as they move quickly through traffic. In this activity, the energizing power of sound is used to "rescue" students from low energy. Try making a loud, moderately high-pitched *eeeee* sound while placing your hand on the top of your head. You will be able to feel a vibration in your skull. Don Campbell tells us that sound is the only tool we have for massaging our brains! It works—playing with sound will "massage your brain" with vibration, stimulate your mind, and give you more energy.

Students can become sirens by using the long vowel sound *eeeee,* swooping the sound as high as they can, then gliding down to the bottom of their range and back up again. A few times making the emergency vehicle siren sounds and student energy levels will have been rescued! (You can also play with the long vowel *aaaaa, iiiii, ooooo,* and *uuuuu* sounds!)

# 17 Moving Energy Infusions

These activities use movement to give students a little more mental energy.

## Activities

### Shake It Off

You know the phrase *blithering idiot?* Well, that's how you feel when you do this activity, but if everyone does it, nobody cares. Spend 30 seconds "blithering," as singer Susan Osborn calls this activity. Start by having everyone stand and shake their hands, then add elbows, shoulders, hips, legs, feet (one foot at a time, please!), and finally the head. Making noise while you blither helps, too. Just let your face muscles go slack and let out a bbblllllbbbllll! You can also suggest to students that they use this activity to "shake off" their problems—imagine the problems falling off their bodies as they wiggle.

### Conducting Your Life

Play a selection of lively, energetic music. Have everyone stand and conduct to the sound! You can suggest that students imagine conducting their way through some part of their lives and add a few goal-setting directions during the selection such as the following:

★ Conduct your way successfully through this week's spelling test!

★ Conduct your way through the end of the semester and finals week!

★ Conduct yourself all the way into the next grade level.

★ Hear the sweet sounds of graduation and conduct them!

When you get to the end of the music, have everyone give each other a round of applause for a great performance!

# 18 Energy March

Play two minutes of march music while students stand with closed eyes. Have them imagine marching through learning tasks with great enthusiasm and success. Use the dynamic power of your voice to create excitement as you lead the imaginary march through various subjects and daily activities. You can use lilting waltz music and imagine dancing through the day as well.

## Body and Brain Olympics

Play a lively music selection and lead students through a few minutes of jumping jacks and other aerobic movements to get their blood flowing. Now have students close their eyes and imagine their brains exercising, building up thought muscle to use for the next class project. When the music is over, let students know they are ready to win their gold medals in social studies (or whatever subject you are moving on to).

> How does one become a butterfly? You must want to fly so much that you are willing to give up being a caterpillar.
>
> —Paulos

# 19 Energy De-Fusers

These short interludes have the ability to diffuse, or de-fuse, energy, as the case may be. These activities are relaxation techniques that you can use to bring students' high energy into balance. It's important for students to learn to recognize when they need to calm themselves and just as important for them to have effective techniques that help them relax. If you find that students are not responding to an energy de-fuser, however, switch gears and run out some of the energy with an energy infuser (student energy may be too high to de-fuse). Sometimes you will be more effective running students' energy on high for a few minutes 'rather than trying to force bottled-up energy just to go away. The key is to get students to focus and direct their energy for a moment and then steer the focus toward classroom studies. If you can do so, you'll have a lot of positive, high-energy focus on learning!

Sometimes students (and teachers) just need a warm fuzzy to bolster spirits. You can also use these activities to lift spirits. You can accentuate the relaxation effect in any of these activities by playing quiet, comforting music in the background.

## Activities

### My Favorite Things

Have students close their eyes and imagine one of their favorite things, such as raindrops on roses, whiskers on kittens, the snug warmth of their bed, a refreshing jump into a cool lake on a hot day. You can select a student to share his or her favorite thing each time you do this activity and have the entire class imagine the student's favorite thing, which is a great way to get to know each person a little better as well as to relax the class.

### Breath Balance

Ask students to close their eyes. Now have them breathe in and out slowly six or seven times. Direct the rate of their breathing. You can also suggest that students breathe out any tension or bad feelings they might have and inhale warm air that brings a sense of peace and calm into their bodies.

### Reach for Stars

Have students close their eyes and imagine they can see the stars in the night sky. Now have them see one particular star that represents something they would very much like to have or to be. Ask them to open their eyes, stand, and reach up, up, up toward the stars, stretching as high as they can. When they finally reach their special star, have them grasp it with a hand, pull it down from the sky, and place it in an imaginary basket on the floor. You can repeat the exercise, having students stretch with the other arm. Continue star-gathering until students have focused their energy, stretched their muscles, and gathered enough stars for a lifetime! Use breathing to assist in this exercise by having students blow out all the air from their lungs as they bring the star down from the sky to the floor. Ask them to inhale deeply as they straighten up and reach for the next star.

### Relax My Bones

Often children don't know exactly what we mean when we say "Slow down!" or "Calm down!" Although children may want to please us, they don't always have the skills to do so. Educator Dee Coulter tells a story of a high-energy little boy who found a clever way to slow himself down. When she asked him what he thinks about when he calms himself, he replied, "Oh, I just relax my bones." This child's wonderful, creative mental imagery allowed him to key into an effective technique for slowing down.

You can conduct a tension-release relaxation activity based on this imagery. Have students stand, shrug their shoulders as high as they can, and hold this position as tightly as they can to a count of ten. I call this "tightening your bones," and I have students hold their breath during the count. On ten we "relax our bones," release the body tension, and let all our air out. Everyone gets a kick out of tightening all the facial muscles because doing so creates great facial expressions, and it feels good, too. After you have held the face tension for a moment you can tell students to relax their faces.

### Dead Weight

In this activity students relax their bodies by using the imagery of being lifeless. Have each student find a partner, and if you have room, ask one partner in each pair to lie down on the floor and become "dead weight." You can also have the dead-weight students sit on the floor or on a chair while the "living" students sit or stand behind the dead-weight partners. Each dead-weight partner becomes as limp as possible. The living partner will pick up one of their "dead" partner's arms and gently move it back and forth, up and down. The dead-weight partner is to let the arm be as heavy and limp as possible. Caution the dead-weight students against pushing against their partners' hands—the weight comes from limpness, not pressure. The living students can also move their dead partners' heads back and forth slowly or rock the dead partners' torso from one side to another if the dead partners are sitting. Have partners switch roles.

44

# Who Am I? Naming Myself

April Moore

One of our first answers to "Who am I?" usually comes in the form of the names given us by our parents. At another point in our lives, we may answer by saying we are students, teachers, butchers, bakers, candlestick makers. We may refer to ourselves as mothers, fathers, single parents. Our identity may be focused on calling ourselves "A" students, or we may see ourselves as special education students or school dropouts.

Although we all know we are more than the labels we are given or take on, an understanding of the many ways we have of naming ourselves will help us recognize how many things we are and can be. The following activities explore our identities through name, fame, and frame.

# 20 Who Am I? Image-Streaming

Image-streaming is a technique for visual thinking developed by Win Wenger at his Institute for Visual Thinking. Image-streaming has been highly successful in helping students improve their learning in a variety of curriculum subjects. I have used Win's method as a brainstorming technique to allow students to bring out many of their feelings, knowledge, and assumptions about themselves. Students enjoy this quick and easy technique and you may want to explore its use for classroom subjects as well.

## Activity

Tell students that they are going to take a look at the images they hold of themselves through a technique called image-streaming. Have students find partners and sit close enough so they can hear one another's voices. One student will be the "imager" and the other will be the "listener." Ask students to select their roles.

Tell your students the following:

> *When we begin, imagers will close your eyes and describe any and every image you have about yourselves, even if it seems unimportant. Describe your personal images to your listeners so that the images are as real as possible. Provide as much detail as you can. Tell your listeners how your images of yourselves look, smell, feel, and sound; tell the emotional aspects of yourselves, the names you have for yourselves, your hopes, dreams, goals, and everything you are aware of. The image-streaming will last for one minute. The only rule is that imagers cannot stop talking but must speak about their personal images constantly for the entire minute.*

*The listeners' role is simply to listen qui-*
*etly to everything your partners say. When*
*the minute of image-streaming is up, partners*
*will switch roles and the listeners will become*
*the imagers and image-stream about their*
*personal images.*

When students have selected their roles, ask the imagers to close their eyes if it will help them image-stream. (Some students may not feel comfortable closing their eyes; I never insist that they do so.) Tell them to begin and have them talk to their partners for one minute. Ask them to stop after the minute is up and switch roles. Your students now have quite a bit of information about themselves, some of which they may never have verbalized before. Now is a good time to continue with another activity that reinforces students' personal images. Have each student write a paragraph about her or his personal image, make a mind map or list of personal characteristics, or write a letter to her- or himself that describes the image. You may want to repeat this activity later in the year to let students explore changes in their images.

# Flying Further

The use of image-streaming can become a natural part of any course of study. Image-streaming takes very little time and lets students know how much information they already have about a topic. The following are related activities that you can use in any curriculum area. You and your students will find other applications for image-streaming as you develop this technique.

★ Use image-streaming to introduce a new subject or idea, to create curiosity about new objects or equipment, to review recently learned material, to assist in recall of information learned at a previous time, or to provide a technique for insight into personal issues.

★ Image-stream following a demonstration or experiment; image-stream about a scientific process such as a volcanic eruption, photosynthesis, the process of uplifting mountains.

★ Set the scene of a historical moment and image-stream about the event; become a historical character and image-stream about his or her role in history (especially how the character feels about that role).

★ Image-stream about life in another country.

★ Image-stream about compositions or art work; image-stream about a composer's or an artist's life.

★ Image-stream everything in students' awareness as they move step by step through a problem to a solution.

Another interesting application is to pre-question subject material. Ask students to image-stream about an object or idea before you explain it. For example, give students a sedimentary rock and have them image-stream about it; show students a violin and have them image-stream about how it is played and what it sounds like; show students a picture of a foreign country you will be studying and ask them to image-stream about the scene; pass a starfish around the room and have students image-stream about its life in the ocean.

The students will gain greater benefits from the experiences if you provide time to synthesize and review the images to understand the overall meaning. A good way to synthesize is to create a group mind map of all of the ideas and images that came up during the image-streaming.

# 21 Metaphor Names

Clinton Lentz

Our names are among the first sounds we recognize as words. Although we respond to our names when someone says them, we may not particularly like our names. They may not be the names we would have chosen if we had been given the opportunity to select. We may not feel that our names represent us very well.

In this activity students give themselves metaphor names, names that create mental pictures that are extensions of their personal self-images.

## Activity

Many American Indians have names that create images. I have friends with names such as Running Bear, White Calf, Yellow Kidney, and Heavy Runner. These names were given to them when they were born. Take a name survey and see how many students like their names. How many students feel their names suit them? There is, of course, no right or wrong answer to these questions.

Tell students they will have the opportunity to give themselves a metaphor name, a name that reflects part of themselves. They should be careful to choose names they feel truly represent them. In this activity, I have named myself "Woman of the Wind" because I play many wind instruments and music is one of my strongest and best-loved life experiences. My students understand immediately why the name has meaning for me. You may want to give students a day or two to decide upon a name. When students have selected their metaphor names you can have them share their names with the rest of the students, explaining why they chose them. Have students write their metaphor names on construction paper and tape them to their desks. Ask students if they would like their metaphor names to be used as occasional alternatives to their given names.

# Flying Further

The following are related activities that you can use in art and language arts.

- ★ Have students create symbols that reflect their metaphor name.
- ★ Ask students to write creative stories about how they have earned the right to their metaphor names.
- ★ Have the students make pictures of themselves doing activities that reflect their metaphor names.

# 22 I've Been Framed!

This activity gives students a chance to determine the different aspects of their lives that they feel are important parts of their self-images. They can "frame" themselves with these associations.

## Activity

Ask students to make collages with pictures showing all of the things they like to do, things they feel are a part of them, and their dreams, hopes, and goals. Students can use pictures from magazines, photographs of themselves from home, or drawings they make themselves.

When they have finished the collages, ask students to bring good-sized photographs of themselves to school. If a student does not have a photograph, take snapshots of students or have them draw self-portraits. An alternative to a picture is to have students write their names in large letters on a piece of paper.

When the students have pictures or other suitable representations of themselves, have them take their pictures and "frame" them with the collages. They can glue their pictures on top of the collages. Or have students put their collages face down on a table, lay their pictures on the back, and trace around the edges of the pictures. Now have students measure and draw lines that are 1/2" smaller than the size of their pictures. Cut the smaller rectangles out of the collages and tape the pictures to the back of the collages so that the pictures show through the frames. Hang the pictures where everyone can see them.

> Life is something like this trumpet. If you don't put anything in it you don't get anything out. And that's the truth.
>
> —W.C. Handy

# 23 Personal Symbols

David Brewer

Our identity is often connected with objects that have become symbols we accept as part of who we are. Some of these symbols, such as our names, are given to us. Others we choose for ourselves. Symbols can portray our interests and say something about who we feel we are. In this activity each student will have an opportunity to select something in his or her life that has special importance and create a symbol for it.

## Activity

Discuss symbols and brainstorm or mind map various symbols in today's world (the symbol for the Olympics, trade logos, the dollar sign, political party symbols, and so on). Ask students to reflect quietly for three or four minutes on what is most important in their lives at this time. When the students have had enough time to reflect, ask them to think of a symbol that can represent the meaning of this important aspect. Give the students time to draw their symbols. They can share the meaning of their symbols with the class or a friend if they like.

# Flying Further

The following are related activities that you can use in English, social studies, history, science, and art.

★ Have each student draw four things that symbolize his or her life from birth to the present, with each symbol representing a turning point or important event. Let each student share the symbols with a friend.

★ Lead students through a guided imagery in which they go to a special nature spot and find a personal symbol. Make sure you provide time for them to explore fully whatever they find. After the imagery ask students to share their personal symbols and their meanings with a friend.

★ Ask students to experiment with writing a letter or short paragraph about an event using picture symbols instead of words.

★ Research hieroglyphics and have students draw their own hieroglyphs.

★ Have students determine what symbols have been used by people throughout time to represent important events or aspects of life. Ask them to make a chart showing these symbols.

★ Ask students to research the symbols used in science and each draw one.

★ Make an art collage or picture using only symbols.

# 24 Four Square

This activity is a way for students to look at themselves through other people's eyes. It also gives students a chance to formulate their own self-images.

## Activity

Give students an 8-1/2"-x-11" sheet of paper. Ask them to draw a horizontal line across the middle of the paper and a vertical line down the middle so there are four even-sized rectangles on the paper. The students will write or draw (or both) descriptions of themselves based on the following views:

★ how I view myself

★ how I think others view me

★ how I would like to view myself

★ how I would like others to view me

Give students plenty of time to complete the pictures or descriptions. I often use circle drawings as these do not require drawing skills but do provide insight.

Discuss the different views. Do students think people see them the same way they view themselves? Why or why not? What can students do to make these views more similar? Is the view that students have of themselves similar to the way they would like to be viewed? How can they make these views match?

Students can share their four views with a friend, post them on a bulletin board, or put them in a special journal about themselves. Have the students keep the pictures and reflect on them later to see if their views have changed.

# 25 Wearing Hats

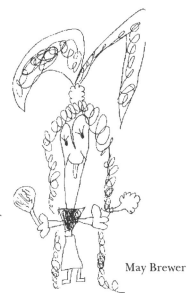

May Brewer

We often hear the phrase "putting on a different hat" when we are reflecting on the various roles everyone has in life. In this activity students will have fun making hats to fit their current and future roles in life.

## Activity

Discuss with students roles that people fill in life. Have the students list the various roles that their mothers or fathers play: worker, parent, husband or wife, member of clubs or organizations, and so on. Ask students to list the roles they play: son or daughter, brother or sister, friend, student, member of athletic team or band, and so on.

Next, have students make hats that reflect each of their current life roles. Have students list the responsibilities that come with wearing each of the different hats. How does it feel to wear these different hats? What happens if you have too many hats to wear? Ask each student to make a hat that reflects a role he or she hopes to fill in the future. What will the responsibilities be then?

## Flying Further

The following are related activities that you can use in history, art, social studies, and language arts.

★ Have students trade hats and share how it feels to fill another person's role.

★ Have each student make a hat that reflects an important role various people have held in history—an explorer, a ruler, a rebel, a politician, an inventor. Ask students to make a list of the responsibilities that come with wearing one of these hats.

★ Ask students to research what the roles of a student, a mother, or a leader would be like in another country. What would that person's hat look like and what responsibilities would come with it? Have students make a hat and list the responsibilities involved in one of these roles in another country.

★ Ask students to make a hat and write a short story about what it means to wear it—tell them to be creative! Have them make a hat from a society in the future. Have fun.

# 26 Individual Identity Profile

Every person has certain interests and abilities that seem to develop from birth. Howard Gardner has outlined seven abilities that are separate, functioning areas of intelligence within the brain. The educational system in the United States has focused on linguistic and logical-mathematical skills for many years. Gardner has proven, however, that spatial, kinesthetic, musical, and personal and social interaction skills are unique and important intelligences, as well. When students and schools recognize these abilities as important and valuable, students with strengths in these areas will feel greater self-worth.

The following identity profile was designed for parents and children to fill out together. It comes from *Redesigning Education: A Guide for Developing Human Greatness* by Lynn Stoddard (1992). An elementary school principal for many years, Lynn has focused much of his career on building children's self-esteem and allowing them to reach their own unique human greatness.

This profile will help students and their parents gain greater appreciation and understanding of student abilities. Parents and teachers can use the profile to find ways to improve students' weak intelligences and honor their strong abilities.

## Activity

Explain the following to the students:

> *There are many ways that we are "smart" or intelligent. A man named Howard Gardner found seven different areas of intelligence: music, math and logic, words, art, spatial skills, movement, understanding ourselves, and the ability to work and play with others. Each of us has intelligences with which we are comfortable and in which we do well. We all have*

# Individual Identity Profile

For _____

| Name | Grade | Date | Submitted by |

*Please rate your child's strengths in the following areas*
*using the 0–5 scale provided, with 5 being the highest rating.*

|  | 0 | 1 | 2 | 3 | 4 | 5 |
|---|---|---|---|---|---|---|

## Linguistic Intelligence
Verbose—enjoys talking and playing with words
Enjoys writing; is fluent and expressive
Reads a lot for pleasure and information

## Musical Intelligence
Sings, hums, whistles a lot (on key)
Enjoys listening to a variety of music, notices various sounds
Plays instrument; makes sounds; feels rhythms

## Logical-Mathematical Intelligence
Curious; asks many questions
Collects, counts, compares, sorts, categorizes, and studies things
Plays with numbers; enjoys arithmetic "problems"

## Spatial Intelligence
Remembers landmarks, places visited
Knows directions, can draw and follow maps
Enjoys and is good at drawing, painting, sculpting
Is clean, neat, orderly

## Bodily-Kinesthetic Intelligence
Graceful, agile use of body
Expressive with dance, gymnastics, gestures, mime, athletics
Handles objects skillfully; can fix things

## Personal Intelligence
Understands and likes self; controls emotions
Self-confident; plans; organizes; uses initiative, persistence, work
Honesty and integrity; zest for life; thankful; appreciative

## Social Intelligence
Kind; friendly; loving; caring; generous; courteous
Leadership/Followership
Listens attentively; demonstrates empathy/respect
Is sensitive to others' feelings

## General Intelligence
Creative; inventive; imaginative
Sense of humor
Money management/thrift
Hobby or expertise in a particular field of knowledge

*areas that are more difficult for us. No intelli-*
*gence is better than another; they are simply*
*different. If we recognize our areas of strength,*
*we can develop them even more. If we also know*
*which areas are difficult for us, we can find*
*ways to improve them.*

Give each student a copy of the Individual Identity Profile. (The profile is also included in the appendix.) Explain to them that they are to take the profile home and fill it out. Their parents can help remember trends and share insights into abilities. Students should return the forms to you.

When the students return their profiles, you will want to spend a little time going over them and making notes of the results for your own information. You may want to develop a program with each child for working with the intelligences productively in the classroom.

# Community Connections

Eric Hoehn

Fear of being alone in the world is an issue every person faces. The connections we make with nature and with other people can provide us with important bonds that help us move through times of feeling isolated. Watching a sunrise, participating in a cultural activity, or honoring a family tradition can be deeply powerful experiences that create feelings of connection.

These connections are also an essential part of our identity. Some cultures have belief systems in which connections with human and nature communities are strong. In other societies, these bonds are not emphasized and some students may have never experienced dynamic cultural ties or developed meaningful relationships with nature. The activities in this section explore community connections in human societies and natural communities. The activities also help to build group identification within the classroom.

# 27 Friendship Webs

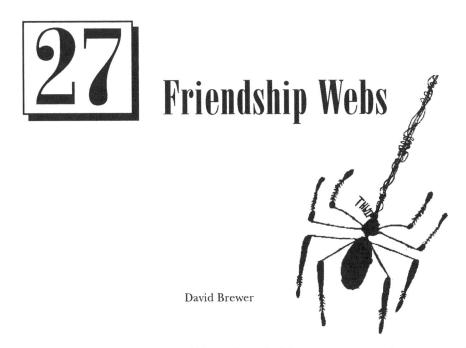

David Brewer

One American Indian tradition views Spider as a weaver that weaves the beautiful designs of life in hundreds of intricate patterns. The spider's body is shaped like an eight, which is the shape of the scientific symbol for infinity. The spider represents the infinite possibilities of creation. Spider's legs represent the directions on the medicine wheel and the spreading of her creative influence everywhere.

We sometimes see the spider as a creature to be feared. The native tradition views Spider's web as the wheel of fate as well as the web of life. We can get caught in the web of fate if we do not take responsibility for our lives. Should we find ourselves in misfortune on the wheel of life, we must take action to change our position. If we do not, we can end up hopelessly tangled in the misfortunes of the web of fate, consumed by our own fears and limitations.

Our community of friends is also like a spider's web. Each friendship is a unique connection, a bond between two people that is similar to a silky strand in a spider's web. The networks of friendships between people within a community weave together to form a beautiful and intricate web of community. The strength of the web comes from the strength of each connection within the web, and every friendship within the network is an important link.

This activity explores the webs of friendship within a community. Students will learn about the strength of friendship networks and may be surprised to discover the number of connections that exist within a community. Students may also realize that the friendship bonds we make put us into different places on the web of life; some are positive and some take us into regions where we do not wish to be.

# Activity

Share the native people's view of Spider with the students. Ask students for their views about spiders and spider webs.

Have students draw large spider webs on pieces of paper and write their names in the centers of the webs. Explain that the human community contains many interconnected webs. We are at the center of our own webs but connected to many other webs of human community. Each of the bonds that we make with a person is a silky strand that links the human community together.

Next, have students weave their friendship webs. Each can start by writing the name of a close friend as a connecting strand from the center toward the outside of the web. Ask them to think about the other people that this friendship connects them with; have them write the names of these people as additional threads that lead to the outer rounds of the webs. For example, through one of my close friends I have made four more casual friends and have also made connections with my friend's parents and three siblings. My friend's mother works at one of the local stores. I sometimes go there with my friend and so I know the other people who work in this store. The close bond with my friend has led me to twelve additional human connections that are all part of my human friendship network. Have students explore their networks of human connections. There will be room on the webs for a number of different close friends and networks of connections.

When students have completed their webs, put all of the friendship webs on a bulletin board and title the display "Web of Human Community." Don't be surprised to find that the web somehow manages to extend to other places around the world. Discuss with students how widespread our human connections are and reflect upon the importance of the human community web.

# Flying Further

The following are related activities that you can use in science, ecology, art, and social studies.

★ **Reflections:** Allow students time to browse through art books that contain photographs of well-known artists' works depicting friendship. Look for Winslow Homer's *In the Mowing* and other works depicting the interaction of friends by Norman Rockwell or Mary Cassatt. How do these artists' drawings reflect friendship? Ask students to reflect on what they feel is special about a friend. As a class, brainstorm and mind map words that define friendship.

Provide appropriate art materials and have children draw or paint their own pictures about friendship. Display the artwork in the classroom or make a gallery for the hallway or library.

★ **Animal Friends:** As a class, in groups, or through individual reports, explore the social structure of wolves, whales, ants, bees, geese, cats, apes, and other animals or insects. Ask students to pay special attention to whether or not the animals play together or seem to be friends. How do animals rely on one another? Which animals live solitary lives? See if the students can find photos or video clips that show animals together.

Through class discussion, compare notes on animal relationships. Do animals seem to nurture and care for one another? If so, how do they show their friendship? Do they compete or fight? If so, why? In what ways are the animals' relationships important to their survival? How are human relationships important to human survival?

★ **Friendship around the World:** Ask students to research various cultures' ideas of friendship. Students can ask children from cultures other than their own what is important in their culture about friends and if there are special ways children form friendship bonds. Is the definition of friendship different around the world? Ask students to share their findings with the class or to write a report. As a classroom project, create a "Friendship around the World" mural or collage.

★ **Spiders:** Study the biology and ecology of spiders. Research what spider webs are made from and how spiders make them. Go for walks to look for webs. Find library books about the different kinds of spiders and their webs. Read stories about spiders and have students write their own stories about them.

# 28 Heritage Treasure Hunt

Some families and cultures place a great deal of importance on heritage, tradition, and lineage. For others, the significance of these family connections has faded. Most people who rediscover information about their heritage also find a new sense of identity. Suddenly history comes alive, people in the past have new meaning, and today's people feel connected in a new way to the cultures of their ancestors. Jean Houston conducts a powerful activity in which participants reach behind them and imagine being connected to their ancestors while reaching in front of them and imagining a connection with future generations. The feeling of being in this far-reaching connection forward and backward through eons of time is a dynamic experience.

The Heritage Treasure Hunt is a treasure hunt in which students must find out information about their family history and bring the information back to the classroom to share. This activity is a beginning point for students to reflect upon their heritage. It is also a valuable opportunity for students to share heritage stories with one another. The students who have strong heritage connections will be able to communicate to other students the strength of the cultural and family identification they experience. For some students this activity may be the first time they make heritage connections. These students are usually somewhat in awe of the students who are so firmly grounded in their heritage. You may even find students who know nothing about one of their parents or whose families are not supportive of this activity. While this may be disconcerting at first, you can redirect these students' energies into exploring the cultural history of their strongest cultural connection. Assure students who have been adopted or live with foster parents that it is just as valuable to study the heritage of *their* culture. Often children with loose or unknown family ties find reassurance and a sense of inclusion by making general cultural connections.

This activity is also a great way for students to learn more about one another and is a good project for early in the school year.

# Activity

Give students copies of the Heritage Treasure Hunt List below and have them bring back answers to as many questions as possible. (The list is also included in the appendix so you can copy it more easily.) Have students share their findings with one another. This sharing is an excellent opportunity to open a class discussion about different cultures and the differences among the cultural traditions of class members.

## Heritage Treasure Hunt List

1. Where was your father born?

2. Where was your mother born?

3. On a map, locate where one of your grandmothers lived when she married your grandfather.

4. Find out how the family of your grandfather celebrated the birth of your father. (What traditions were prominent in the culture of your grandfather for celebrating the birth of a child?)

5. What was your mother's or father's favorite food as a child?

6. On a map, trace the path of your father or grandfather through all the different places he lived.

7. What language did one of your great-grandmothers speak?

8. Ask your grandmother to sing one of her favorite childhood songs and write down the words. Or see if your mother remembers a song her mother sang to her.

9. Find out which of your family's traditions was passed down to your family by a grandparent.

10. What is the history of your family name? What country is it from? Does it have a specific meaning in the language of this country? Has the name been changed?

# Flying Further

The following are related activities that you can use in geography, social studies, English, and art.

★ Make signs representing the continents and put them around the room. Have students stand where their mother's mother lived and then move to where their mother grew up. Do the same for fathers. Note trends in migration movements.

★ Make lists showing the various languages spoken by each student's ancestors and the favorite foods of each student's father or mother.

★ Have an international food fair and ask students to bring in a food sample and recipe of a traditional food in their culture or family.

★ Ask students to write a short biography of one of their grand parents.

★ Have students draw a family tree.

# 29 Moving Connections

This activity explores the movement and dance styles of various cultures. The movements of a culture say a great deal about the character and attitudes of a society. The restrained, contemplative movements in a reflective Asian dance tell us as much about an aspect of their culture as do the energetic hops and swoops of an African dance. And what do the flamenco dances say about Spanish society or the kicking jigs say about the Irish? When we actually move like the people of another society we gain deep, intuitive insight into the feelings of another culture.

There are entire cultures of people whose sense of self-esteem has been taken away by a dominating culture's attitudes and actions toward them. Many of the children in the less-dominant cultures would never dare to imagine they could move freely like the children of the dominant culture. These people (including adults) live with the daily reminder of what has been impressed upon them as a symbol of their supposed inferiority: the color of their skin or some other characteristic that sets them apart.

Although these attitudes are changing, the transition is slow and will require great effort to manifest. We can make progress by teaching children new attitudes of respect and understanding for different cultures. When we have walked in someone else's shoes, when we have moved, thought, and felt like the people of another culture, then we may begin to understand, honor, and work together as a global society, holding each culture in esteem and cooperating to create a safe, high-quality, and meaningful life for all of Earth's peoples.

## Activity

Explain to students that they are going to explore the movements and music of different lands. In this activity, students will not be learning the traditional steps of these ethnic dances, but will improvise movements that have the appropriate flavor of the country's movement styles. There is a surprising feeling of authenticity in these movements.

Play music from one of the countries listed and demonstrate or read the movement styles of each country's dances to the students. Suggest that the students let the music lead them in their movements. You can also use some of the simple instruments that are used in each country: drums, rattles, bells, tambourines, maracas, and guiros are common percussion instruments the music room may have available. Although it would be optimal to have a large room with lots of moving space, I have done this activity successfully in rooms where the students had to stand next to their desks.

Next, switch to another country and experiment with the appropriate movements. It is good to give students a chance to talk about the differences, similarities, and feel of these sometimes new ways of moving.

## Cultural Movement Styles

Some of these ideas were developed by Teresa Benzwie (1988); others I got when I participated in a creative movement workshop in Seattle with Anne Green Gilbert. If you have students who are strongly entrenched in a culture not included here, you may want to add their culture and a description of its dances to the following list.

**AFRICA:** African dances use movements of hips, undulating movements of the torso, and strong, direct movements of the body, especially the arms and legs. The people in these cultures use drums and rattles.

**INDIA:** Indian dances involve intricate hand movements, small foot stamps, and turns of the head to focus the eyes in different directions. The people in this culture use bells.

**VIENNA:** Vienna is famous for the waltz. Any large, flowing movements around the room that coincide with the three-beat pulse would be appropriate. It helps to teach students the foot movements of the waltz.

**AMERICAN INDIAN:** Many American Indian cultures use small, stamping movements and bend their upper torsos forward. They often dance in circle formations. Many Americans Indians use gourd rattles, drums, and bells.

**SPAIN:** Spanish dancers hold the upper body very straight and erect. They use large, controlled arm movements high in the air and out to the sides. They dance with quick, small steps without moving the legs far from a normal standing position. They use castanets and clap their hands.

**SOUTH AND CENTRAL AMERICA:** Traditional South and Central American dances have a lot of variety that includes rapid hip action, large arm movements, and fast, whole leg movements. Dancers use maracas, rattles, guiros, and wood blocks.

**CELTIC IRISH:** Traditional Irish dancers use lively leg and knee movements. They use drums.

**HAWAI'IAN:** Hawai'ians use large hip movements and graceful, undulating arm movements to the sides. Dancers also hold their hands in front of their bodies and use "sign language" to tell a story.

# Flying Further

The following are related activities that you can use in history, social studies, physical education, and music.

- ★ Ask students to imagine what they would be wearing to dance to the music of a specific country: boots, bouffant pants, a billowy skirt, ribbons, flowers? Research the traditional dance costumes of a country. Have students share a picture, make their own costumes, or draw a picture of the traditional clothing.
- ★ Have students explore the traditional dances from the era of your history studies. Ask students to write a report, draw a picture, or mind map the characteristics of the dances and clothing.
- ★ Teach students traditional cultural dances. Students or their parents may know some traditional dances and may be willing to share them. If the dances arouse students' sincere interest and curiosity, it can do a great deal for raising the self-esteem of the student who has a chance to share his or her cultural heritage.
- ★ Study the differences between the dance music of two countries. Listen to musical selections and see if students can recognize the differences.

# ⟦30⟧ Tree Connections

Matt Butterfield

Feeling a part of the natural world is an important identity connection that inspires us to recognize what wonderful and unique creations we are. We can appreciate with awe the grandeur and beauty of the sky, waters, air, and mountains and become fascinated with the intricacies of the minute details in nature. The plant world offers us many levels of understanding. To stand beneath a towering redwood is to appreciate the majesty of trees. The global movement to save the live-giving South American rain forests has brought new attention to the important role trees play in maintaining air quality and atmosphere balance. You may have read Shel Silverstein's book *The Giving Tree*, which points out the many ways in which people use trees. American Indian peoples, among others, have special reverence for plants and their gifts. Contemporary mainstream medical practices still use plants or what they have learned from plants to create medicines. Holistic medicine uses many plants in their gentle, natural form to assist in healing.

This activity gives students the chance to explore natural connections with trees (even if there is only one in your neighborhood). If students have never sat beneath a tree and derived comfort from its solid presence, or climbed a tree and sat cradled in its limbs while watching the world from this elevated vantage point, then this activity could be a doorway to finding comfort, connection, and courage within nature.

# Activity

Ask students to look around at one another and decide which two people in the class look the most alike. As the group discusses similarities and differences, note that no two people are really alike.

Next, lead students to a place in the schoolyard or nearby where there is a group of trees or at least two trees. Compare the bark, limbs, height, color, texture, and leaves of two trees and note their differences. Share with the students that no two trees are any more alike than any two people in the class. If there are many trees close by, tell students that they will be going on a journey to get to know a tree.

Have each student find a partner. One person closes his or her eyes or is blindfolded and is led by the partner to a tree. The partner with closed eyes explores the tree fully by touching it and is then led back to the group meeting area. Tell the blindfolded students that they can open their eyes and look for their trees. If students have difficulty finding their trees, they can be aided by clues of "you're getting warmer or colder." Give them time to examine the trees with their eyes. (Interestingly, once students have explored a tree thoroughly, they often "befriend" the tree and go back when they need time alone or time to think.)

If you have only one tree nearby, give all of the students a chance to get to know it. Have them close their eyes and feel its bark. Have them stand or lie beneath it and look up at the limbs and leaves. Let them examine the minute details of its bark, leaves, flowers, or fruit. Ask them to be aware of the smells of the tree. Does the bark have a taste? If you can determine its age, make a time line of all of the things this tree may have seen in its years. Tell students to find five minutes when they can sit by the tree alone and feel its presence.

# Flying Further

The following are related activities that you can use in science, art, ecology, social studies, and language arts.

★ Students can research different species of trees. How are they different from one another? Ask students to make a list or draw pictures of some of the different tree species found locally. You can tell what species a tree is by its shape and color when you stand far enough away to see the whole tree. See if students can determine what clues will let you know the species of local trees.

★ Have students find out about the different parts of trees, draw a picture of a tree, and label the various parts.

★ Ask students to research the different ways that humans use trees and the different things trees provide for humans. Make a list or a mind map.

★ Have students find out how trees function in the hydrosphere, biosphere, lithosphere, and heliosphere. Students can make diagrams, write reports, or draw pictures to illustrate the role of trees in these natural systems.

★ Find three different kinds of wood and share how the wood is similar or different in its color, density, and usefulness to humans and animals. See if students can determine how the differences among the trees from which the various woods come affect the wood characteristics.

★ Have students research the current status of trees and forests on Earth. How is this valuable resource being managed? Where are the problems the greatest? What are the implications of improper forest management? What are some solutions to the problem? How can students help with the solutions? Ask students to write reports answering one of these questions.

★ Have students find out how different cultures honor and use trees; have students share their findings.

★ Explore artists' work that highlights trees or forests. Have each student pick his or her favorite work and share it with the class. Ask each to make a drawing of a tree.

★ Ask students to find pictures or photos of trees. What does the tree seem to represent in each picture? Trees with leaves, fruit, and flowers seem to be offering gifts and new life, while the barren tree in winter may speak to us about survival. Have students write a few words about what the trees in their pictures seem to be conveying.

# 31 Life Form Forum

Sheena Wolfe

In this activity, students select plants or animals to represent, make masks of the life forms they have selected, speak about the life forms' relationships to Earth and other creatures, and provide information on the current ecological status of the life forms. The activity can be used in science, ecology, and art.

This is a very powerful activity that brings students a greater awareness of the struggles of life forms in today's world. With all of the human interference and pollution, Earth has become less hospitable to life forms than it used to be. Students make a strong mental, emotional, and spiritual connection with the life forms on Earth in this activity and also realize that survival is a struggle for all creatures. Studying animal survival techniques can also give students ideas about how to survive in difficult situations. Sometimes this recognition will give students who have difficult lives an emotional boost.

You can integrate this activity easily into science and ecology studies.

# Activity

Begin by telling students that the class will hold a forum, or meeting, focusing on the life, needs, and problems that all kinds of life forms have in today's world. Each student can select a plant or animal to represent in the forum (don't forget bacteria, algae, slime molds, and other small life forms). Give students time to make a mask of the life form they represent. They can make their masks from paper bags or plates and decorate them with string, sequins, yarn, feathers, and other ornaments.

Ask students to research the life form they have selected. They will find out about the life form's relationship to Earth, to other life forms, and especially to humanity. Ask students to imagine what the world would be like if this particular life form were not on planet Earth today. Have students prepare a statement that might be spoken by this life form if it could talk. They should include comments about the life form's biology and ecological role, and should request changes in the environment that could improve its living conditions.

When all the students have prepared for the forum, have them bring their masks and reports and sit in a circle. Ask the students to put on their masks and, one by one, present their statements from the life form. Ask them to say who they represent and to speak as if they were the life form addressing the group.

# CHAPTER TWO

# Reaching Out: Making Connections

*There's a rhythm in the flow of our lives each day;*

*There's a rhythm in the patterns of our work and play;*

*There's a rhythm in our walk;*

*There's a rhythm in our talk;*

*There's a pattern that connects me to you,*

*And we can find the rhythm between the two.*

*There's a pattern that connects me to you,*

*And we can find the rhythm between the two.*

—Chris Brewer

If life were a journey each person traveled alone, people would probably find it an interesting but lonely experience. But life is not a solitary jaunt. Life's paths are crisscrossed by the footsteps of many people, and being able to join with others on life's paths is important to each traveler's self-esteem.

People sometimes appreciate life events that they share with other people much more than those events they experience alone. A sharing relationship, however, can also bring sadness and conflict. Like a teeter-totter, the interaction between people constantly fluctuates between harmony and disharmony, action and reaction, resonance and frustration.

Life itself includes both heights and depths. Life would not be a fulfilling journey if its paths did not lead us through the full human experience of joy and sadness. It is often from the depths of despair that we gain our greatest insights, as well as an appreciation for the heights of joy. There can be no thrill to the ride on the teeter-totter without going both up and down.

We cannot expect that life be an experience of continual happiness. Nor can we expect relationships to remain harmonious and joyful all the time. We can, however, move past the rocks and ruts on life's journey with greater ease if we have the skills that are necessary to keep the movement balanced and flowing smoothly. When we find the perfect rhythm on the teeter-totter, the balanced flow is a thrilling experience. And when we find a relationship that has a rhythm and balance, we have made a memorable human connection.

Skills for listening, expressing, and communicating can provide us with ways to keep the ups and downs of our relationships flowing. Without the ability to listen carefully or express ourselves clearly we may find it impossible to stay on the relationship teeter-totter. The activities in this section will help students build skills for listening, expressing, and communicating, giving them confidence in themselves and their abilities to form fulfilling relationships.

Knowing and experiencing successful relationships is one of the essential aspects of self-worth. Each person has an inner world of feelings, hopes, experiences, and fears. When we communicate with others we gauge just how much of our inner world we can share safely. When we risk letting someone see into our inner world and it proves to be a place she or he would like to visit again, we feel worthy. Our sacred inner world has been seen and deemed valuable. When other people allow us to meet them in their inner world, we feel worthy; they are trusting us to be in this very special place. The bond that is formed when two people's inner worlds have been shared is precious. This bond needs to be protected, however, through attentive listening skills, the ability to express ourselves honestly, and careful understanding.

Use the activities in "Reaching Out" to help students form relationship bonds, keep relationships healthy with good communication skills, and find rhythm and balance in the teeter-totter of relationships.

# Listening

Emily Cummings

Listening—the act of reaching out to understand another person—is the bridge from our inner worlds to the outer world. Listening is so basic to communication, learning, and life, that it may very well be the most important skill we can develop. In a sense, our listening skills are really a listening intelligence that dictates much of our success in the outer world.

Listening is very different from hearing. We cannot keep from hearing and being affected by the sounds around us. But when we listen, we are actively involved in an intentional act, a purposeful reaching out for sounds, with a desire to understand another individual.

The way in which we listen, the way in which we are willing to enter into the sounds around us, determines what our experience will be. We can listen mentally to the content of the words that are spoken or we can listen intuitively to the messages the body sends through its movements and stance. We can listen for the emotional meaning in the tone behind the words or listen to the spirit and intention of the thought.

The more ways in which we are able to listen, the greater will be our appreciation of and benefits from an experience. The more ways we can teach students to listen intently and attentively, the greater will be their learning rewards. The following listening activities are only starting points for helping students develop a listening intelligence, but the activities provide examples of basic listening skills that you can develop throughout the curriculum.

# 32 Soundscapes

Emily Cummings

This activity helps students to tune into active listening, or as the Latin phrase for listening, *ob audire,* expresses, to "reach out" for sound. Learning to listen well is a skill that takes time and practice to develop. Just taking the time to experience listening to sounds intently is a good starting place. Soundscape listening is a foundation for developing the listening attentiveness necessary for good interpersonal communication.

The concept of an auditory landscape or soundscape is explained and used in the Energy Cycle Circle activity in chapter 1. You may want to use these activities together.

## Activity

Read the following explanation of soundscapes to your students:

> *We are surrounded by sounds! We awaken to familiar sounds, listen to music we enjoy, endure unwanted sound over which we have no control. Familiar, routine sounds orchestrate the structure of our day, while new sounds bring exciting accents and rhythms to our inner world. This*

*symphony of sound creates a sound landscape
or soundscape, a term coined by music educator
R. Murray Schaefer to define our auditory
environment.*

*Every person has unique soundscapes. For some,
a morning soundscape might include the local disc
jockey on the early shift signaling the time to rise,
while the pattering of the water in the shower calls
attention to the onset of the day and the whistle of
the teapot and beep of the microwave herald a
greeting to the stomach. For others, a morning
soundscape might be insistent nagging, "If you don't
get up, you're gonna be late!" while bacon sizzles,
and kids fight over who gets to go into the bathroom
first.*

*When we stop to listen and become aware of
our sound environment, we develop the skill of
attentive listening, an important tool in living and
learning. The following activity assists in this
process.*

Have students sit quietly for a few minutes and listen carefully to the sounds around them. Discuss the sounds your students heard.

Explain the concept of soundscapes. Ask students what soundscapes occur regularly in their lives. What sounds are a part of these soundscapes? What is a playground soundscape like? A school bus soundscape? How about a student's after-school home soundscape? Have students compare their after-school soundscapes at home to the soundscape at a friend's house.

Have the students make a mind map of some of their daily soundscapes. You can assign students to identify various soundscapes at home and to make lists or mind maps of these soundscapes to share at school. The purpose of this activity is to get students involved in active listening.

# Flying Further

The following are related activities that you can use in language arts, history, and science.

★ Have students individually choose soundscapes to explore and write down the sounds from their soundscapes, being as descriptive with their sound words as possible: rrrrring! beep, beep, beep, pppsshhhhhh. In groups of four, have each student re-create the sounds from his or her soundscape and see if the other students can guess what the soundscape is.

★ Ask students to tape record sounds at home and share them in class. Can the other students guess what the sounds are?

★ Have students write a poem or a prose piece about a specific place and use descriptive writing to explore the place through its characteristic soundscape.

★ Explore a history soundscape from the current curriculum studies—the crossing of the Delaware, the battle of the Little Big Horn, the first Independence Day. Divide the students into small groups and have them create a soundscape by using mouth sounds to depict the historical sounds (flowing water, people paddling a boat, gunfire, horses' hooves). The groups can share their soundscapes with the class. For extra fun, the groups can keep each soundscape a secret and see if the other students can guess the historical event behind the soundscapes.

★ Have students use large appliance boxes to make a nature sphere for each of Earth's systems: a heliosphere, atmosphere, lithosphere, hydrosphere, and biosphere. Students can decorate the outside to identify the sphere characteristics. They can make the inside comfortable enough for others to sit in and experience the sphere. Ask students to create a tape recording of sphere sounds that can be played while students are inside.

When I did the last activity with seventh- and eighth-grade students, the results were astounding. The atmosphere had wind sounds with a fan blowing on the students inside. The lithosphere was a volcano eruption, complete with sounds and people to shake the box from the outside. Even the principal had to crawl on his hands and knees through the hydrosphere, decorated with hanging fish and other sea creatures!

# 33 | Listening Clues and Cues

There are different ways we can listen to people when they speak. One way is through the content or meaning of the words. Another is through the emotional tone of their voices. The third is by observing what the body says through its movements and stance. This activity explores these three ways to listen and teaches students to become sensitized to hearing what others are saying through body, emotion, and words.

## Activity

Experiment with various forms of voice and body expressions by asking students to repeat the messages after you, using the appropriate emotions and movements in the Natural Expressions list that follows. (The list is also included in the appendix so you can copy it easily.) Students should mirror your vocal and body expressions. For young children, you may want to start with vocal expression only and then add body movements.

Ask students to form groups of four and give each group a copy of the Natural Expressions list of words, emotions, and body movements. Have students take turns in their groups saying the statements and expressing the words with the corresponding emotion and body movements until they have read all ten examples.

Next, hand out the Mixed Messages list and ask students to read the same statements using the emotions and body movements listed. Students may find they have to practice movements and vocal expressions separately first. In fact, the incongruence makes this activity very difficult and you may end up just laughing the attempts away.

When students have finished their expressions and movements, ask them to share what it was like to hear the words spoken with an emotion and body movement that didn't fit. Was it difficult for them to make the statements with the mixed physical and emotional expressions? Discuss how much of our communication is nonverbal and how we can listen sensitively to a person through vocal tone and body movements.

## Natural Expressions

| Content Message | Emotion | Body Movements |
|---|---|---|
| I love to eat apples. | joy | lively |
| My foot hurts. | pain | restless |
| I am really upset about what happened. | anger | tense |
| I don't like to go into the hall when it is dark. | fear | cringing |
| I'm concerned about getting home late. | worry | jittery |
| I feel uncomfortable about eating the candy. | guilt | nervous |
| I wish my dog hadn't died. | sadness | limp |
| I can't believe I said what I did! | embarrassment | timid |
| I know I can pass the test! | confidence | strong |
| I'm so glad we can go to the circus! | happy | energized |

## Mixed Messages

| Content Message | Emotion | Body Movements |
|---|---|---|
| I love to eat apples. | pain | restless |
| My foot hurts. | joy | jittery |
| I am really upset about what happened. | happiness | limp |
| I don't like to go into the hall when it is dark. | guilt | strong |
| I'm concerned about getting home late. | confidence | lively |
| I feel uncomfortable about eating the candy. | fear | energized |
| I wish my dog hadn't died. | embarrassment | tense |
| I can't believe I said what I did! | anger | cringing |
| I know I can pass the test! | sadness | nervous |
| I'm so glad we can go to the circus! | worry | timid |

# Flying Further

The following are related activities that you can use in language arts and drama.

★ You can make this activity into a game by making message cards green, emotional expression cards red, and body movement cards blue. The students randomly draw one card from each category and then perform the words, movement, and emotional expression they have drawn. Students enjoy the spontaneity of this game.

★ Have students create their own messages, body movements, and emotional expressions. Use the creations in the class activity or make game cards. To help students build communication skills, you can ask them to make up a combination about how they feel or how they felt during a particularly memorable event (good or bad).

★ Make a list of adverbs and adjectives as part of a language arts lesson. Have the students come up with an accompanying message and body movements that would reflect the meaning of the modifiers. Ask students to perform their messages with the movements and see if the class can guess the emotional modifier.

★ Cut out pictures from magazines of people with strong facial and body expressions. Have the students write a caption that sets a scene and names an emotion for each picture.

★ Find three newspaper comic strips that are fairly uncomplicated but have a strong visual message. Eliminate the words from the captions. Pass out copies of the cartoons to the class so that each student has one cartoon. Ask the students to write their own captions that reflect the facial expressions and body language of the cartoon characters. Post the results. This activity can be great fun and works well with adults, too.

# 34 Copycat Listening

Mae Clark

All children play the game of copying everything someone else says, usually to the frustration of the person being copied. In this activity, students will play the copycat game and then use reflective listening to help build interpersonal skills and vocabulary. Young students may have a more difficult time with their reflective listening, although they do the copycat listening eagerly.

## Activity

Ask students to find partners. One student is to be the storyteller and think of something that happened recently that she or he would like to share. The student might also describe a family member or pet. The storyteller writes down five or six sentences she or he wants to share about the topic and tells the story, one sentence at a time. The partner repeats, word for word, everything that the storyteller says.

The storyteller repeats the story. This time the partner uses different words that mean the same as the words the storyteller is using. If the story is written down, only the storyteller should look at what is written. For example, the student sharing the story says one sentence, such as "I went to the lake yesterday." The other person then repeats what his or her partner said in a slightly different way: "Yesterday, I took a walk down to the water." The first student continues: "Since I didn't have my swimsuit on I couldn't go in." The other student might say something like, "I didn't wear anything to swim in so I stayed on the shore." The conversation continues until the storyteller's story is complete. The partners then trade roles and repeat the activity. Note that the partner uses first person statements to paraphrase what the storyteller says.

When students have each told a story, tell them that in reflective listening, the listener doesn't give or share new information but helps the other person to hear what he or she is saying by paraphrasing. Paraphrasing helps to affirm that the feeling is okay, encourages further sharing about the feeling, and assists students in learning to express themselves accurately. The listener may also reflect the feelings she or he thought were in the statement by asking questions. Sometimes it is appropriate to encourage the speaker to explain feelings more by asking a question such as is shown in the following example:

| | |
|---|---|
| **First student:** | "Susie is a real jerk!" |
| **Second student:** | "You don't seem very happy with Susie. (paraphrasing) Did she make you feel angry?" (question response) |
| **First student:** | "She left with someone else when we were supposed to go down to the store together!" |
| **Second student:** | "She left you?" (paraphrasing) |

Ask students to share something about a feeling with their partners. Emphasize that it is important for the listeners to paraphrase what the speakers are saying to bring out what the listeners think the speakers are feeling.

# 35 Emotional Baggage Porters

May Brewer

The co-counseling technique, originated by Harvey Jackins, provides an opportunity for a person to express feelings and issues without fear of judgment. The technique is valuable because it allows people to get their feelings out, and they can often change negative and debilitative emotional baggage into positive, constructive action.

This activity is invaluable in teaching students to become good listeners and friends. The listener makes very few or no comments. It is important, however, that the listener show support through attentive listening skills: maintaining eye contact, holding the body in an active listening position, and truly listening to what his or her partner is saying.

Once people have developed co-counseling skills they have a valuable focused listening technique that they can use with family, friends, or in other relationships. This technique can help students release in a safe environment their feelings about troublesome issues. Once feelings that may be preoccupying students are released, students can return with more energy and clearer thinking to learning activities. This activity also promotes caring, kindness, openness, and social thinking skills within the classroom.

# Activity

Teaching children co-counseling requires that you modify the adult technique but use some of the basic concepts. This activity works best when children have the same partners for a time so that they can develop trust in one another.

To protect trust, establish ground rules. Let students know that they are not to repeat or mention anything their partners say again, even to the partners. Students will appreciate that they have this level of confidentiality. Ask them to think of the process as throwing away emotional baggage that no one wants to see or hear about ever again. Students can think of the baggage as gone once they have said it.

Co-counseling partners divide time so that each person has an opportunity to share feelings and to listen to the other. Students should recognize that they are expected to give equal time to their partners, which may mean that they split ten-minute sessions equally, or that they take turns speaking for a whole session.

Explain that sometimes we just need someone to listen to us and a chance to get our emotions out. Often, we can change how we feel once these emotions are out. It's important for students to know that it is okay to feel anger, fear, disappointment, jealousy or other negative emotions. We wouldn't be human if we didn't feel these emotions. It's what we *do* with these emotions that is important. Let the students know that the purpose of this activity is to express feelings, however the students are feeling them, and to "air them out." Like laundry that smells fresher once it is aired out, airing out problems can make one feel better, fresher, and more energized; it gives life whiter whites and brighter brights!

Tell students clearly that they need to develop the following important listening skills:

> **Students should listen without taking sides and without telling their own similar stories. Tell students it is important to listen and be there as an emotional baggage porter—helping their partners get rid of emotional baggage so they don't carry it around forever. The listeners are the emotional baggage porters! And the way to help their partners get rid of emotional baggage in this activity is to help those partners air it out to someone they can trust.**

Children (adults are worse) sometimes have trouble with this activity because they can hardly keep from saying "it's okay" if their partners are upset. For the person sharing, the problem is not "okay" and this person needs to feel that the emotions she or he is feeling are valid. Students should avoid the temptation to say a problem is "okay."

Students should avoid giving advice about the problem. Once the sharer has aired feelings, he or she will get to an appropriate solution.

Students need to be taught that an attentive listener pays attention by focusing on what the other person is saying. Help students understand how important eye contact and body position are in attentive listening.

The rest is simple. Have each student select an emotional-baggage-porter partner. Periodically give students ten minutes to sit with their partners and air any feelings about current issues. Remember to have students take turns sharing concerns. You may also want to provide a special space where students can go to have privacy during class if an issue comes up unexpectedly and they want to share with their partners for five minutes. Be sure to keep the time to a few minutes. And remember that students will think and learn better if they don't have emotional baggage with them!

# 36 Sleeping on Problems

Many times my mother suggested that I sleep on a problem. What she wanted me to do was to think about a problem before I jumped on a solution. Often, when I had given myself a little time to sleep on a problem, I gained new insights, listened to the other side of the issue with more clarity, and ended up resolving the issue differently from the way I might have had I not taken time to think about it.

This activity combines my mother's adage with a perception-checking technique called "pillow talk." Perception checking is a way of listening to other people's interpretations of an issue and checking how an issue looks from all points of view. The pillow talk method described by Paul Reps was developed by a group of Japanese school children. It is called pillow talk because a pillow has four sides and a middle, just like problems.

In pillow talk, there are four positions each person considers when she or he is working with a problem that involves a dispute. When an issue has been perceived from these four positions, the resolution of the problem occurs with respect for each person's viewpoint. Usually the resolution involves some form of compromise, or at least the problem is resolved with understanding and appreciation for all sides of the issue.

This activity is a good tool for teaching students how to listen to another person's viewpoint and develops a communication skill that will be invaluable throughout life.

Following are the four positions:

**Position 1:** I'm right, you're wrong.

**Position 2:** You're right, I'm wrong.

**Position 3:** We're both right and both wrong.

**Position 4:** It really isn't important who is right and who is wrong; the issue isn't as important as it seems.

**The conclusion:** There's truth in all perspectives. (The conclusion is the middle of the pillow.)

# Activity

Ask students to think of a disagreement they have had recently with a friend or family member. Have them write the problem down in one or two sentences and, if the problem has been resolved, ask them to write down how the problem was resolved. If it hasn't been resolved, ask them to write down how they would like it to be resolved. Have the students write how the problem looks from each of the four pillow-talk perspectives. After they have looked at the problem from these perspectives, have them write how they would choose to resolve the problem now. Students compare this solution with the solution they had before the exercise. Are their solutions different? Are their feelings about the other person different? Has the exercise helped them to look at the problem through the other person's eyes?

Students will need to do this activity a number of times to develop it into a skill. You can have the students practice this technique by using it as a way of resolving classroom disagreements or you can periodically ask students to use it with whatever issues are currently bothering them. The Flying Further activities also give students practice while giving them opportunities to think about, or sleep on, some of the political and social issues of our time and throughout history.

# Flying Further

The following are related activities that you can use in current events and history.

- ★ Use the four perspectives to look at current conflicts, such as control of Palestinian lands. How should the apartheid issue in South Africa be resolved? How should the issue about dolphins and tuna nets be resolved? Who should pay for major accidental oil spill cleanups?
- ★ Use the pillow talk method to look at historical conflicts from various perspectives .

> A journey of a thousand miles begins with one step.
>
> —Lao-Tzu

# Expression

Jason Robinson

On the bridge between our inner and outer worlds, at the opposite end of listening, is the ability to express oneself. Without personal expression, we live only in the inner world. To reach the outer world we need to communicate our thoughts and feelings. But expressing ourselves can be a frightening experience. Expressing requires that we share a part of who we are, opening ourselves to criticism and the approval or disapproval of others.

There are many ways in which we can express who we are. We communicate our personality through sound in both the words we speak and the emotion in our vocal tone. The very word "personality" comes from the Latin word *persona,* which means "through sound." Our movements and actions also speak for us, and creative art forms are expressions of our inner world, as well. In fact, every aspect of our lives expresses in some way who we are. Finding effective means of self-expression is important to being understood, to feeling that we have been heard, and to communicating wants, needs, and issues.

I often tell private music students that the only way they will learn to play their instruments well is to explore the full potential of those instruments. Any creative endeavor or personal expression is the same. The body, voice, and emotions are all tools for expression. In order to know how to really "play" the human instrument to its greatest expression, you have to explore its boundaries.

We need to explore boundaries so we know our potential and our limits. We have to go the edge of our boundaries and fall over occasionally in order to know where the edge is. When we have fallen over our edges, we at least know how far we can safely go. Push to the limits, learn where the edges are, and we will know where we can go!

The following activities give students opportunities to explore their boundaries safely.

# 37 | Opposites

By exploring opposites, or extremes, in many different ways, we can find some of the edges of personal expression boundaries.

## Activity

I have done this activity with students in grades four through eight. We first use movement to illustrate words that express opposite meanings. Then students select an art medium to make an illustration of the opposites. I am always amazed at the intuitiveness and deep expression of feeling that is exhibited by the students' artwork. Younger students studying opposites in language arts will also benefit from these activities.

Ask students to stand where they have space to move. Give them a pair of words with opposite meanings and ask them to use their bodies to express first one of the words and then the other. Here are some suggestions:

| round | straight | | hot | cold |
|-------|----------|--|-----|------|
| sit | stand | | fast | slow |
| small | large | | near | far |
| freeze | melt | | up | down |
| push | pull | | yes | no |
| wide | narrow | | tall | short |
| left | right | | loud | soft |

Ask students to explore emotional opposites. Following are some suggestions:

| | |
|---|---|
| sad | happy |
| nervous | calm |
| angry | pleased |
| confident | worried |
| begrudging | generous |
| fearful | courageous |
| rebellious | compliant |
| discouraged | hopeful |
| excited | bored |

Have students each select a pair of word opposites from the steps above and develop an art project around it. A variety of art mediums may be used: clay, markers, oil pastels, or shadow boxes. The students will decide how they can show an example of the opposites in their artwork.

# Flying Further

The following are related activities that you can use in language development, vocabulary, science, art, and physical education.

★ Have students think of their own opposite words and write them on the board. Play movement music and have students create an opposites dance by miming the opposites as you call them out. Students can work with partners; one partner mimes one word and the other mimes its opposite.

★ Teresa Benzwie (1988) adds a therapeutic aspect to the opposites activity. She gives students a metaphor for the opposite movements, such as "push all your cares away," and "pull toward you all the good things you deserve." You can ask students to help make up movement metaphors for any of the opposite pairs.

★ Ask students to think of as many opposites in nature and science as they can and write or draw them. Share the opposites with the class.

# Sound Expressions

I have a friend who is a chiropractor and has done quite a bit of work with interpersonal communications. She once told me a story about a woman at a workshop. The woman stood up and told the workshop leader that her daughters had difficulty expressing anger and asked if he had any ideas that could help. My friend said that the woman stood very stiffly and her voice had absolutely no emotional inflection when she spoke. The key to the daughters' problem seemed obvious from the mother's behavior. The workshop leader replied, "Well, how do YOU express your anger?" The woman said nothing but merely sat down. I hope that she recognized her own difficulty with expressing herself and that she had probably never taught her daughters HOW to express anger.

If you have never gone swimming, chances are that you will need to get into the water and flounder around before you get an idea of how to use your body. Using your voice to express feelings is much the same. You just have to experiment to see what your voice can do. The next three activities explore vocal expression by experimenting with various textures, vowel sounds, pitches, and emotions.

# 38 Sound Expressions: Toning the Voice

la la la

David Brewer

Here is an opportunity to explore texture, pitch, loudness, and softness of the voice. People are often afraid to make sound. How many times at home and in the classroom do we tell children to be quiet? Certainly there are times when children need to be quiet. I have found, however, that adults generally tend to be nervous around children's busy chattering and noisemaking and often demand silence when the sound making is an important part of positive play or learning.

Teachers are often afraid that if the classroom is not quiet the sound will be a poor reflection upon their abilities to discipline their students. But there is a time and place for quiet. We know through recent research that simply listening to someone lecture is one of the least effective ways of learning. Sharing, moving, experimenting, experiencing, and talking are all effective learning methods and most of these make noise. Play is indeed child's work, as Piaget said, and play makes sound!

There is another advantage to this invigorating and entertaining activity. The vibration of the sound stimulates the brain and you will probably find that you all feel higher energy levels after you have done this activity. Ask your students how it makes them feel. Because sound stimulates the mind, the activity is especially appropriate before doing tasks that require concentrated effort. In addition to the stimulation of vibration, the activity brings more oxygen to the brain through the increase of breath. The high frequencies in the sound and the amplification of these frequencies at close range also stimulate the electrical charges in the brain. (For more information on sound production and brain stimulation, see Brewer and Campbell 1991.)

This activity offers students a chance to make sound and experiment with using their voices—an activity they may rarely get!

# Activity

Stand with your students in a fairly tight circle (you may want students to link elbows). Have everyone release three or four loud sighs on the vowel sound *aaaaah*. Select a pitch in the middle of your students' range and have them sustain this pitch with the aaaaah sound. Switch to making the vowel sound *eeeee* in a high pitch and continue with this sound for one minute. Tell your students to breathe whenever they find it necessary. Using the vowel sound *ooooo*, sing a low pitch and sustain it for one minute. Experiment with the long vowel sounds *iiiii* and *uuuuu*. Ask students to try different pitches freely while using any vowel sounds. Continue for at least two minutes or longer.

For another exercise in toning the voice, see Sound Emotions in chapter 1.

# 39 | Sound Expressions: Emotional Nonsense

A person's voice is a reflection of her or his emotional state. When we are happy, our voices are rich and vital. Sadness creates a low-pitched, dull-sounding voice that lacks energy. Anger, fear, excitement, suspicion, and curiosity all have unique vocal characteristics, as well. This activity helps to develop an awareness of emotional expression within the voice.

## Activity

Gibberish is a nonlanguage language. It is a combination of sounds that have no meaning.

Read the following gibberish poem to your class three times: the first time using an angry voice, the second using an excited voice, and the third using a fearful voice. After each reading, ask students to guess which emotion you are expressing.

Oomapoli

Aso mata boomera zu

Frapoli fufu ee hoo-lululu

Umani, pumani ick ick von gick

Ala shoop ala shing ala suma baloo

Razaly roo ona ee ee magroo

Hacow nee oof ees homa baloo

Soto nunu om apoli goo

Eiya zoozoo, om apoli stu.

Discuss with your students how much communication occurs through tone of voice rather than words. Ask students to read the poem, letting other students guess which emotion they are expressing. I have used this activity with groups from kindergarten through adults and everyone seems to enjoy it. Students through junior high seem to delight in the opportunity to read gibberish poems themselves.

# Flying Further

The following are related activities that you can use in language development and reading, history, science, and social studies.

- ★ Ask students to use only nonsense syllables or the alphabet or numbers to talk with one another for one day when they are not doing class work. At the end of the day, have the students share what the experience was like. Were they still able to communicate their thoughts?
- ★ Instead of having your students read history, science, social studies, or literature silently, have them read assignments aloud to a partner using a tone of voice that expresses anger, fear, joy, or excitement. Ask students if they felt that they remembered more because of the emotion in the voice.

# 40 Sound Expressions: Gibberish

Gibberish that reflects an emotion requires a great deal of intonation, facial expression, and gesture for the communication to be effective. A variety of ways to explore communication through emotional voice quality and gesture follow. Use the other Sound Expressions activities as warm-ups for these gibberish activities.

Some of these ideas were developed by Teresa Benzwie (1988).

## Activities

With a partner, have students create a gibberish argument. One person can begin by making an emphatic gibberish statement. The partner responds by loudly gibbering back. The gestures used in this activity are especially important for communicating the argument.

In a group of five or six, ask one person to begin a story using gibberish and to exaggerate the vocal expression. After making a few gibberish statements, the first student passes the story on to the next person and so on around the group. Tell students to imagine what is happening in the story. When everyone has contributed to the story, let students share the story lines they "heard" in the gibberish tale.

Have students use gibberish in an invented party. They can walk around the room, talking to different people individually and in small groups. Students don't necessarily need to know what they are saying. Ideas for a conversation "theme" will come up spontaneously and students can expand on these ideas.

With the students' help, think up and write three or four two-sentence conversation themes on the chalkboard. Have students "speak" these sentences with one another using gibberish to convey the meaning. Students can continue the conversation, expanding along the same line of thought. The examples of themes that follow were created by a fourth-grade class:

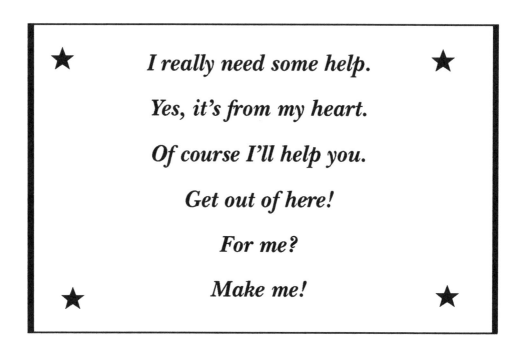

*I really need some help.*

*Yes, it's from my heart.*

*Of course I'll help you.*

*Get out of here!*

*For me?*

*Make me!*

In groups of three, have two students develop a gibberish conversation while the third student "draws" the conversation using colors, lines, and shapes to express what he or she hears in the conversation. Ask students to give their conversation artwork titles. Students can rotate roles.

Use these activities to stimulate students' thoughts for a creative writing project. After students have had gibberish conversations, ask them to write a short story based on an idea they may have had during one of the gibberish conversations or stories.

# 41 Clipping Hedges

"Say what you mean and mean what you say."

Whitney Baldwin

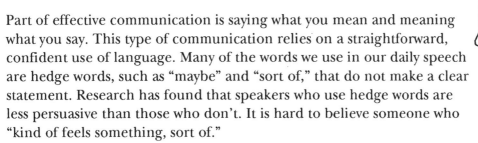

Part of effective communication is saying what you mean and meaning what you say. This type of communication relies on a straightforward, confident use of language. Many of the words we use in our daily speech are hedge words, such as "maybe" and "sort of," that do not make a clear statement. Research has found that speakers who use hedge words are less persuasive than those who don't. It is hard to believe someone who "kind of feels something, sort of."

Believing in yourself also means that you believe what you feel or think is true. Here is an activity to help students recognize how their choice of language can give the listener a feeling of either confidence or uncertainty.

## Activity

Explain to students that some language reflects an attitude of believing in yourself and other language expresses self-doubt. Ask them how they would feel if you told them that "cell walls are sort of permeable, maybe" or that you "guess that verbs are action words, don't you think?" While it's important to leave room for discussion of certain issues, it is also important that people speak from the best of their experience, be clear about how they feel and what they think, and be flexible enough to listen to new ideas.

Write the following list on the board:

# HEDGE WORDS

sort of

kinda

maybe

I guess

probably

uh

well

er

Don't you think . . .

I probably shouldn't say this, but . . .

I'm not really sure, but . . .

I hate to say this, but . . .

Make a class project of clipping hedges to reduce self-doubting words. Here are a few ways to clip hedge words:

★ Post the list of hedge words on a bulletin board.

★ Pick a hedge word each week and focus on removing it from the language used in the classroom.

★ Play "hedgehogs" by having everyone try to hog as many hedge words as they can. Every time a student hears someone using a hedge word, the student calls out "hedgehog" and gets one point. At the end of the day, the person who has the most points is rewarded. (The trick is trying to figure out how to reward a hedgehog!)

★ Focus on removing hedge words from students' writing. Circle hedge words each time you find them in writing assignments and have students replace them with clear statements.

# 42 Trying Times

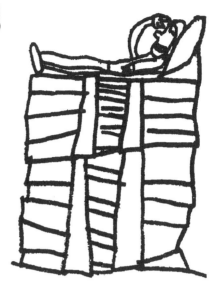

Devin Schmit

This activity also looks at the effects of the words we use to express ourselves. Carla Hannaford, educational kinesiologist, shared this idea with me. It comes from Paul and Gail Dennison's (1986) educational kinesiology methodology.

"Try" is a struggle word. It doesn't mean to *do* something, it means only to attempt something. For example, try raising your right hand; don't *do* it, just try to do it. Does this discussion boggle your mind? Well, the truth of the matter is that the word "try" does boggle the mind. Educational kinesiologists can show you how the word try will "switch off" the brain because of the imprecise and conflicting meaning of the word. "Try" does not encourage you to accomplish something, it does not support you in the belief that you *can* do what is asked; it only suggests that you *might* be able to do something.

What words might you use instead? The Educational Kinesiology Foundation suggests that you use "do your best." This supportive statement asks you to *do* something and then encourages you to do it as well as you can! "Do your best" also lets you know that your best is okay. You do not have to match someone else's goals.

## Activity

How often do we use the word "try" in our communications? Experiment with keeping track of how many times during a day you hear others or yourself ask someone to try something.

# 43 The Truth Drink

The activities listed below use words to help students express themselves, distinguish truth from lies, learn more about each other, or learn curriculum material in an enjoyable way. This is a good activity for developing a greater understanding about the consequences of statements and actions. The Flying Further activities help students listen for and recognize verbal and nonverbal cues.

## Activity

Have students pretend that they have a magic drink. When they give it to someone, that person has to tell the absolute truth, the whole truth, and nothing but the truth for one hour. Have students write a short story about how they might use this truth drink and what might happen if they did.

## Flying Further

The following are related activities that you can use in history, social, studies, arithmetic, science, literature, and drama.

★ Have students imagine that the truth drink makes them tell the truth two-thirds of the time. When they drink it, they will tell the truth twice, but lie once. Sitting in a circle, have students share individually two things about themselves that are true and one thing that is a lie. See if the other students can guess which is the lie. This activity is good to do in the beginning of the year because it helps students get to know one another.

★ Give students one or two pages of reading from the science, history, social studies, arithmetic, or literature texts. Be sure that you give each student a unique page or pages. Ask students to select two facts from their reading that are true and make up one fact. Have students share the three items with the class and see if the other students can guess which is not true. You can divide the students into teams and make this a game: have a student from one team share his or her facts and give the opposite team a point if the team can guess which fact is false. If the guessing team doesn't guess the false fact, the other team gets one point. This method offers students a way of studying and memorizing information while they have a chance to explore verbal   and nonverbal cues.

★ Give each student a paper bag that has an object in it. One by one, have students bring out their object and exclaim: "Oh, my long lost _____ (name of object). This is my favorite object because . . ." Students are to improvise an explanation of why the object is their favorite and how it got lost. Often, a part of a stu-dent's background will come up as a true aspect of the story. Have students share any part of their story that is true. Students can learn more about each other through this activity.

> **If you know where you want to go, you have a much better chance of getting there.**
>
> **—Anonymous**

 **Opinionated Art**

David Brewer

This activity helps students to recognize the value of their opinions and to honor the opinions of others. The Speaking Up activity also helps to develop confidence in personal opinions.

Many of the world's well-known artists have expressed their personal opinions about political and social issues by drawing or painting statements of their feelings. Students can learn a great deal about expressing opinions by exploring the works of these artists, taking the time to develop their own opinions about an issue, and deciding how to depict their thoughts visually.

# Activity

Explain to the students that there are many ways to express an opinion. Brainstorm with students the various ways people can express themselves. Share books that show works by artists such as Winslow Homer (Civil War paintings), Norman Rockwell (paintings that reflect daily life and social issues), Pablo Picasso (especially the Massacre in Korea, the War and Peace painting, and the Guernica mural), Diego Rivera, and other artists who have used political or social issues as subjects for their material. There are some wonderful contemporary artists who have created dynamic works about current global issues, such as peace and ecology. Give students time to browse through the books and reflect on the artists' statements.

Ask students to think about an issue that is important to them and to make a drawing or painting that reflects their thoughts and feelings about the issue. The issue can tie into current studies on political events, social studies, history, or ecology. Have students share their art in the class or put up a gallery in the hallway. The artists should write a two- or three-sentence explanation or poem that explains their opinions about the issue.

# 45 Speaking Up

Bobbi Jacobsen

Learning to develop and honor our own ideas and opinions is an important part of building self-worth. Speaking up and sharing opinions are also important to being a contributing part of a community. This activity explores the process of researching and evaluating an issue, making a decision about the issue, and writing justifications that support and defend a position. You may want to find articles on a current topic that students can explore for opinions.

This activity has been adapted from an activity developed by Merril Harmin (1992).

# Activity

Ask students to spend fifteen or twenty minutes reading through current local newspapers and magazines. When students have found issues that interest them, ask them to research the issue at home, the library, or in the classroom reference materials. Ask students to decide what their opinion is about the issue and write a short supportive statement about their opinion. If appropriate, students can send their opinions to the local newspaper's editorial column. As a class project, students can also contribute their statement to a published classroom issues and opinions paper for the class to read and share. As an alternative to a letter, students may write and deliver a news commentary.

# Communication

Where the paths of listening and expressing meet, the bridge of communication is formed and relationships begin. When the act of expressing is met with attentive listening, communication becomes meaningful. Trust and friendship can emerge when a bond of understanding is formed. The word *friend* evolved from *freond,* an ancient Germanic verb meaning "to love." Communication requires entering into another's inner world, which we must do carefully and lovingly. The reward is permission to return to and become acquainted with the inner world of another person.

Communication can be made through mental, physical, emotional, or spiritual modes of expression and listening. These skills can be learned through interactive activities in the classroom. Cooperative learning techniques are invaluable for teaching communication skills. In the activities that follow students will have an opportunity to explore positive relationships and various forms of communication.

# 46 I've Got to Hand It to You!

People often "talk" with their hands, using them to emphasize a point or express a feeling. Here is a chance for students to explore the magnitude of communication possible through hand movement. This activity is also a good way for students to release pent-up emotions. It is especially beneficial for shaking off unnamed feelings because the activity eliminates the burden of having to find words to express feelings.

## Activity

Ask students to sit on the floor with partners close enough so they can touch each other's hands. Using *only* hands, ask students to greet one another.

Ask the students to let their hands express happiness. Then ask students to express the emotions listed below, letting students know when to take turns doing a hand expression and when to do them at the same time:

> let your hands be shy
>
> have your hands express anger
>
> let your hands play together
>
> have your hands say you are disappointed
>
> let your hands express how you feel when you get an A on a school project

have your hands say you are sorry

let your hands tell a story about an important
    memory

have your hands tell your friend how much
    you appreciate him or her

let your hands show how you feel right now

# Flying Further

★ Do a hand study: Cut out pictures of hands from magazines and make a collage or write a few sentences about what you think a particular pair of hands is expressing. Look for pictures of hands from different cultures; hands working, playing, caring for others; hands that are young, old, or in-between; hands that are hurt, healthy, healing hands. Hang the collages up for a hand-some gallery!

★ Have students spend an hour working in the classroom on group projects but tell them to use only their hands to communicate. Have them share what the experience is like.

★ Have students make a list or mind map of the different things that hands do.

★ Expand the activity to include conversations between partners. A student makes a hand movement to state something. The partner responds with a movement. The partners make statements to one another and ask each other questions. Students can move through space to make a movement point if they need to. Students can create an entire story or situation spontaneously. When students are finished, have the partners share the experience verbally. You can do this activity with three or more partners.

★ Give students face paint and have them paint their hands. Hands can become faces of people or animals, plants, or just decorations!

★ Use feet to explore communication in the same way.

# 47 Tell Me More

Devin Schmit

Our society teaches that we shouldn't be proud of our accomplishments, much less talk about them. Modesty, though important, often gets in the way of positive reinforcement and recognition, sometimes keeping us from doing things well.

As a child I had great difficulty accepting a compliment. When someone said something nice about me, I would deny their compliment and say something like "Oh, no, I'm not really very good at that." One day, my best friend gave me a compliment, got my usual denial, and in frustration said somewhat angrily, "Why don't you just say, 'Thank you'?" I was astounded that it could be that easy. After that exchange I did just say "Thank you" when someone complimented me, but I found it very difficult to do at first. When I could finally accept compliments well, I realized that I could also honor my own abilities and strengths.

Tell Me More is sometimes difficult for people to do, but it usually helps students overcome compliment denial. The activity also teaches that a compliment is a gift to be honored and that the person who gives it deserves to be thanked for taking the time to notice something positive. People who experience Tell Me More often learn how to GIVE more compliments, too!

## Activity

Ask your students to participate in a short, enjoyable experiment. Ask them to respond to the next compliment they receive by saying "Thank you," and then adding, "Say, why do you like my . . . ?" or "What is it you like about how I . . . ?" The point is to ask the compliment-giver to tell them *more* about what it is she or he likes. Usually, the person who gives the compliment is happy to tell your students more; students get the benefit of knowing more about what they did right and feeling better about themselves. They can always say thanks again and explain the class experiment. Usually everyone gets a chuckle and students get the warm fuzzies from the additional explanation.

# 48 Making a Statement for Yourself

When we are upset with someone most of us will make a statement about what has upset us. Although we may not mean to, these are often blaming statements similar to those that follow:

*You always . . .*

*How come you can't . . . ?*

*I wish you wouldn't . . .*

*You said you would . . .*

While these statements may be true, a criticism that starts by inferring that someone did something wrong immediately puts others on the defensive and may also make them feel bad about themselves. If another person feels defensive, he or she may respond in self-defense, say something negative, and pretty soon you have an argument.

If we were to explore a problem we have with someone using the pillow talk method described in activity 36, we might find that other people have good reasons for behaving in certain ways, even if that behavior upset us. Even if we don't agree with these reasons, we may still get better results if we reframe critical statements in ways that clearly state how we feel but don't blame the other person. People are more receptive to making a change if they don't feel they are being attacked.

Such a statement shows that you share your concern from the standpoint of how you feel about what's happening, stating your complaint as "I feel . . . " For example, the complaints above could be reworded as, *"I feel* like there are a lot of times when you . . . *and I'm not very comfortable* with it." *"I would like* to see you . . . " *"I would feel better* if you didn't . . . " *"I get upset* when you say you will do something and you don't."

114

The important point of an "I feel" statement is to say how the other person's action makes you feel and not to blame that person for the action. When you use "I feel" statements you are being more honest about the situation than if you were to use a blaming "you did" statement. A complaint is, after all, an expression of how you feel; the other person may not feel the same way or may not even know that what she or he is doing is a problem for you. If people hear that their actions make someone else feel uncomfortable, they are often willing to adjust their behavior. Even if people aren't willing to adjust their behavior, you have presented an opportunity for them to state how they feel about the issue (since you've stated how you feel) and the two of you can begin to find a compromise.

When you make an "I feel" statement you are taking responsibility for some part of the problem and also indicating a desire to work with another person to resolve an issue. This cooperative attitude makes the interaction a problem-solving, team effort rather than an angry criticism that states your dissatisfaction and infers the other person is wrong.

An "I feel" statement also gives the other person more information because you are being specific about what bothers you, not just saying that the other person makes you mad. When you say "I feel uncomfortable when you . . . " the other person has some idea of what the issue is and what might make the situation better.

# Activity

Explain the difference between "you did" statements and "I feel" statements. Ask students to notice how often they hear or say "you did" statements. Ask students to replace "you did" statements with "I feel" statements. Changing this habit may take awhile, but with reinforcement, the "I feel" statements become a communication habit.

# 49 There's a Pebble in My Shoe

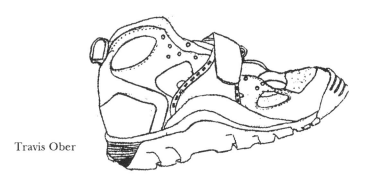

Travis Ober

This activity was developed by Ole Andersen, president of LIND (Learning In New Dimensions) Institute in San Francisco. Ole uses this technique with his staff and I have found it to be a wonderful, understandable metaphor that teaches children to take care of a situation when they first begin to feel uncomfortable.

## Activity

With your students discuss what it is like to have a pebble in your shoe. At first, it is so small you hardly notice that it is there, so you don't bother to take it out. You may even go to bed at night forgetting it bothered you. In the morning, you put your shoe back on without taking the pebble out of your shoe. Soon, you notice it and, after awhile, it begins to hurt, but you may be too busy to remove it. Ultimately, what was originally just a tiny pebble begins to feel like a boulder and you finally stop to take it out. By now your foot may be bruised or cut. The little problem has become a big problem.

Children understand easily that a problem, worry, or upset can be like the little pebble in the shoe. If they take care of it early, the pebble doesn't have to become a boulder. It is easy for children and adults to use this metaphor to address a problem when it first occurs. When you say "I have a pebble in my shoe" you are saying that there is something *little* bothering you. The statement minimizes the issue and relieves the stress of approaching someone with a concern. After all, you have pointed out that it's only a minor problem. People don't seem to get upset when approached with a "pebble." They are usually able to get rid of the pebble and are glad it has not become a boulder!

# 50 Give Me Five

Coming to a consensus in a group discussion can be a difficult, or at least a time-consuming, process. It is usually optimal if everyone can have a voice in a discussion rather than just a few outspoken individuals. Here is the best method I have found to give everyone a voice (or a hand, in this case)! This idea came to me from John Runyon of the Leadership Training Institute in Seattle, who rescued a group of concerned educators in conflict from a rather tight spot by teaching us this method. I have since used it in many meetings and classrooms with great success. Don't forget to use this one at teacher's meetings, too!

## Activity

When you have reached the decision-making point in a discussion, it's time to Give Me Five and get feedback on where everyone stands on the issue. Make a resolution statement about the issue you are discussing and ask for student input. You might say, for example, *"Let's get a reading on how everyone feels about our class's participating in the school recycling project. How do you feel?"* Students give you five, or four, or . . . none.

Here's how it works. If they show five fingers pointing toward the ceiling it means that they feel really good about the decision. Four fingers means they feel good but a little less comfortable than someone with five fingers up; three fingers is a slightly less comfortable rating than four. The rating scale decreases to no fingers, or a closed fist, which is a very neutral position. Students would point their fingers down to indicate discomfort with the project. One finger down is slightly negative, while five fingers down means they totally disagree.

The students put their hands up with their fingers showing how they feel, and you all quickly get a sense of the general feeling toward the project or resolution by looking at the hands. If there are mostly three, four, and five fingers pointing up, you have a solution. If there are a number of neutrals or a lot of fingers pointing down, you may need to reconsider the resolution.

When just two or three people are very uncomfortable with a resolution, you can state that the majority appears to be in favor of the resolution, but you may want to get feedback from those that have shown an unfavorable hand. You don't have to go into a lot of discussion; you can simply honor the feelings of the people who are not comfortable by asking them what is bothering them. Sometimes their responses will cause you to change the resolution, but most often asking for feedback just helps you honor another person's point of view.

# 51 The School Post Office

May Brewer

When teachers at Whitesides Elementary School decided to help their students increase interactive abilities by developing a school post office, they discovered an amazing tool. They found that their intraschool postal system encouraged communication among students, taught letter writing, enhanced students' sense of self-worth, provided an opportunity to show caring and friendship, and encouraged a sense of community.

The Whitesides Elementary postal system used a central mailbox and had a mailbox in each classroom as well as in each support staff department. The teachers encouraged students to write letters to friends, other classes, and staff members. The first few days after the post office opened there was a flood of mail. Staff even had difficulty answering all of the letters and some felt that studies were suffering because of all the time involved in the letter writing. After about a week, however, the post office fever subsided as students became more concerned with the quality rather than quantity of their letters.

As the post office experience continued, teachers were amazed to find that the students were learning to read and write without a great amount of formal instruction. Older students were improving their writing abilities. Students were learning by doing and developing self-reliance. Without being coaxed, assigned, or required to participate, the students were increasing their writing abilities and their feelings of self-worth!

Lynn Stoddard (1992) shared this great communication idea.

# Activity

Help students build a central school mailbox out of a box from a large TV or appliance. You may paint the box, cover it with construction paper, or decorate it in some other way to resemble a mailbox. Ask each class and adult staff members in all departments to build their own, smaller mailboxes.

Develop a rotating schedule for students to pick up, sort, and deliver school mail. Teachers will want to teach students how to write letters and address envelopes. Encourage students to write to

- ★ friends
- ★ someone they feel needs a friend
- ★ cooks, custodians, secretaries, librarians, and other staff to say thank you
- ★ the principal and other staff to share concerns
- ★ other classes to invite them to share special events
- ★ teachers to say how they feel about classroom issues or teaching techniques

Staff can use the mailbox to share special thoughts, suggestions, or comments with students.

# Balancing

Some of the definitions of *balance* include the following: a means of judging or deciding; stability produced by even distribution of weight; equality between contrasting, opposing, or interacting elements; an aesthetically pleasing integration of elements; equilibrium. Balance is as essential to relationships as it is to the bridge that connects two sides of a gaping chasm. For the bridge to function, it must first have structural integrity in all parts. In order to have a solid human relationship, each person must have ways to create balance or equilibrium within. We can bring balance into a relationship with tools for keeping our personal stability.

Like the child's teeter-totter, building a relationship requires the ability to weigh and measure two sides and find an even distribution between contrasting elements. Relationships are dynamic. The need to adjust constantly never ceases, although patterns for adjusting may emerge. The understanding that comes from familiarity with another's inner world can make finding an equilibrium easy. A well-tuned relationship has a balance that can be defined as an "aesthetically pleasing integration of elements."

Use the following balancing ideas to explore personal and interactive equilibrium in the classroom. Teresa Benzwie (1988) provided Balance and Space Flow.

# 52 Imaginings

Allison Tuszynski

Imaginings are joyous, stimulating images that initiate an inner feeling of happiness and warmth as they bring pleasant experiences to mind. Imaginings are reminders of the good things in life when a situation is bleak. Imaginings can also provide a refreshing break from classroom activities and empower students with the energy to continue with school work.

## Activity

Ask students to close their eyes and imagine one of these experiences, giving them a minute or two to savor their images:

★ running as hard as you can with a friend

★ white, billowy clouds floating in a bright, blue sky

★ jumping from a sandy beach into warm, blue water

★ dancing with your shadow on the sidewalk on a sunny spring day

★ billions of brilliant stars on a clear night

★ stroking the soft, fuzzy fur of a young kitten

★ biting into a crisp, juicy apple

- ★ riding a bicycle downhill on a long, winding road lined with trees

- ★ sipping a refreshing drink of ice-cold water on a hot summer day

- ★ watching red and yellow leaves as they float down from the trees gently to your feet

- ★ feeling the warmth of a crackling fire on a cold day

- ★ turning in circles with your arms out to your sides until you fall dizzily to the ground

- ★ laughing with a friend until your sides hurt

- ★ skipping rocks over a clear blue pond

- ★ hearing your favorite song on the radio

Use an imagining exercise whenever you feel classroom rhythm needs a boost. Students can contribute their own positive imaginings to this list.

# Flying Further

The following are related activities that you can use in science, history, and art.

- ★ Use imaginings as a stimulus for artwork and have students draw a picture of how their imagining looked.
- ★ Make a list of "science" or "history" imaginings, using settings from the classroom curriculum. Some examples follow:

## SCIENCE—The Water Cycle

- ★ a clear, cold stream flowing through the woods
- ★ billowy cumulus clouds high in the sky
- ★ a light rain falling gently on your face

## HISTORY—The Settlement of the West

- ★ waving grasses on the prairies as far as your eyes can see
- ★ the excitement of discovering gold as you pan for it in a stream
- ★ the arrival of your wagon train in the land in which you will settle

# 53 Moving to Learn

When our minds and bodies are in balance, our learning becomes easier. This cross-crawl technique evolved from 1930s studies about the developmental importance of crossing the body's midline. Educational kinesiology has expanded this information to develop simple, enjoyable movements and activities that enhance whole-brain learning. These activities make all types of learning easier.

This activity is adapted from an activity designed by Paul and Gail Dennison (1986). It is an important learning tool and a good warm-up in the morning or before difficult learning tasks.

## Activity

Ask students to stand where they have room to move. Play a medium-paced, 4/4 tempo movement music selection from the list or find one from your collection at home. You may want to have students bring suitable recordings from home after you have done this activity in class.

Ask students to move to the music, moving an arm at the same time as they move a leg from the other side of the body. First, touch a raised knee with the hand from the opposite side, then touch the other knee with the other hand, always crossing the midline of the body. You can experiment with other ways to cross-crawl: reaching one arm up while the opposite leg moves out from the body, reaching behind the back to touch the opposite raised heel. Students may stay in one place or move about the room, as you choose.

> Every limit is a limit to be examined and transcended.
> —John C. Lilly

# 54 Positive Points

Think back to a time when you have felt upset, worried, or emotionally stressed. Perhaps you will remember holding your forehead in your hand while resting your elbow on a table. This natural reaction to stress actually relieves tension by stimulating neurovascular balance points. These balance points have been called "positive points" by Paul and Gail Dennison (1986) of the Educational Kinesiology Foundation. When gentle pressure is applied to these points it is possible to attain a sense of calm and to stimulate positive, productive thought. *Brain Gym* by Paul and Gail Dennison (1986) describes this activity and many others that are useful for relieving stress.

You can use this exercise to relax and to release body tension. The exercise also provides an opportunity for students to focus on a feeling or issue that they would like to feel more positive about and helps them envision possible solutions. This activity is also beneficial for enhancing long-term memory and may be a useful break during cognitive studies such as spelling, mathematics, or social studies. If a student is experiencing visual stress from intense book work, she or he can have someone massage the positive points to help relieve eye strain. Students can also use this activity to help them calm down before tests, sports activities, stage performances, or public speeches.

## Activity

Ask students to find partners. One student sits quietly in a chair with eyes closed. The other student stands behind the seated student and very gently places her or his fingers above each eye, approximately halfway between the hairline and the eyebrows. The points should be held lightly with just enough upward pressure to pull the forehead skin slightly toward the hairline. The partner holds this position until the seated student feels all emotional stress is gone. When the first students feel calm, the partners reverse positions.

# 55 Bumping the Blues

"I've lost my head!"

Mickaela Christensen

Here are quick activities for working out negative feelings and revitalizing the mind, body, and spirit.

## Activities

Play high-energy music and have students do the Bump, a popular 1970s dance in which two people bump body parts every couple of beats, varying bumping parts. Read "Oomapoli" three times in an angry voice (see Sound Expressions: Emotional Nonsense). Spend five minutes unloading emotional baggage with an emotional baggage porter partner (see activity 35). Punch a pillow. Jump rope or run around the playground. Create a pleasant imagining and drift into it for three or four minutes. Keep a "Darn it!" doll in the classroom and let students tell the "Darn it!" doll off. Make a drawing that reflects anger. Spend five minutes cutting paper into little pieces. Play with clay; go ahead and beat it, punch it, twist it. Play "And furthermore!" with a friend. Take turns saying silly, angry things to one another and begin each one with "And furthermore!" Pretend you are chopping wood. Use lots of energy and say "Hoo" very loudly each time you hit the wood.

# 56 Balance

The purpose of this activity is to build trust and support between people. As students experience the process of balancing their bodies alone and with other people they will constantly make corrections and adjustments. Share with the students that the physical act of balancing is a metaphor for the many ways we adjust mentally and emotionally to find balance in life.

## Activities

Begin by having students experience balance with their own bodies. Ask them to stand on one foot and find as many ways as they can to move the rest of the body while maintaining their balance.

Next, ask students to find partners and hold their partners' hands or wrists securely. Have students bend their knees and lean back so partners are pulling in opposite directions. Students will find they need to make adjustments to support and balance one another.

Have students experiment with different ways of balancing: holding only one of their partner's hands, crossing their arms, standing nearly straight, squatting very low to the ground. Ask partners to sit facing each other, hold hands, and become a see-saw, swaying back and forth. Ask partners to sit with their backs together and try to stand up by pushing against one another. Have them continue to go up and down together. Repeat the exercise with one group of four students sitting back to back with another group of four. The only contact the two rows have with each other is their backs. The groups of four may find it easier to stand if they link arms and one person gives the signal to begin.

Discuss balance, or give and take, in human relationships. What does it feel like when relationships are out of balance? In balance? What tools can we use to help maintain balance?

# Flying Further

The following are related activities that you can use in art, science, mathematics, and physical education.

★ Fold a paper in half and cut a design on the open side. Unfold the paper and find the perfect balance in the mirror image design. Look for balance in artists' work. Draw a picture that depicts perfect balance.

★ Make a balance beam with blocks or use a measuring scale and experiment with finding balance with object weight. This exercise may also lead to lessons on equal and unequal sets.

★ Discuss how nature creates balance: How does nature balance animal populations? How is water balanced in the hydrologic cycle? What happens when nature gets out of balance? Ask students to find examples of balance and imbalance in nature.

> Security is mostly a superstition. It does not exist in nature. . . . Life is either a daring adventure or nothing.
> —Helen Keller

# 57 Space Flow

This activity, adapted from an activity developed by Teresa Benzwie (1988), helps students and adults appreciate the beauty that occurs when people cooperate and work together. Once participants get going, there is a flow to this activity. Use it as an example of balance in relationships.

## Activity

In this activity, students will be taking turns creating body sculptures in and around their partners' bodies in an ever-flowing dance. For variety, do this activity with groups of three or four, or begin with groups of two and add groups together until the entire class is moving and flowing in the space flow dance.

Ask students to find partners. Explain that within a body sculpture, positive space is the space occupied by the body while negative space is the open space.

Play movement music. Ask one of the partners to use her or his body to form a shape. Ask the other partner to find a space within the sculpture and fill the space in some way: place an arm or leg into an open area between the other person's arms or legs, duck beneath the other person's arms, bend over the other person. When the student has found a space to fill, ask him or her to freeze in that position. The first student will then move away carefully and find a space to fill in the new sculpture. When the new space has been filled and the student is holding this new position, the partner will move and create a new sculpture and so on. This exercise is an ongoing dance of students moving and flowing in and out of the ever-changing shapes and holes of each other's personal space.

# 58 | Putting Our Heads Together

Alicia Reiner

One of the most difficult aspects of relationships is recognizing and allowing for differences in opinions. This activity gives students the opportunity to blend ideas and create a joint drawing. The process requires that students acknowledge and respect each other's creativity and ideas.

## Activity

Ask students to find partners. Explain that each pair of students is going to create a joint drawing. Each student will draw half of the picture. Ask one student in each pair to think of an object and the other to think of an action. Without telling each other what they have thought of, ask students to write their ideas down and then share the ideas with their partners. For example, one student may think of a cat while the other thinks of running. The subject of their drawing will be a running cat.

One student begins by making three shapes or lines on the paper to start the drawing. The partner adds three lines or shapes to the drawing. Students continue taking turns drawing until they both feel that they have completed the project. They may include background art as well.

Share the pictures with the class and discuss how the pictures changed as each person added ideas. Ask students how they feel about the finished product. Note the creativity of the drawings!

# Flying Further

The following are related activities that you can use in history and science.

★ Have each student draw a subject without showing it to her or his partner. Then ask the students to create a drawing using the joint drawing process. When the pictures are finished, compare them. Note the similarities and differences of ideas. Discuss the originality of the pictures.

★ Have students use this technique to draw a picture that illustrates a history lesson.

★ Ask students to illustrate a science concept using the joint drawing process.

# 59 What if . . .

Students who act impulsively often do not think about the consequences of their actions. Accepting responsibility for our actions is an invaluable living skill that we can teach in the classroom by using discipline that stresses logical and natural consequences of behavior. As students begin to recognize the potential consequences of their behavior, they will begin to understand that the choices they make are directly related to the quality of their lives. This activity will help students understand consequences.

This activity also encourages students to explore options for solving problems. An important part of solving problems is recognizing that there are many possible solutions. The more options we allow ourselves to consider, the greater the opportunity we will have to find creative, workable solutions.

## Activity

Discuss the Third Law of Motion, which states, "For every action there is an equal and opposite reaction." Describe how this basic law of physics applies to our personal actions. For instance, ask the students to brainstorm what might occur if they

- ★ ate only candy all day
- ★ helped with housework
- ★ never did their homework
- ★ came home very late after school

Make a mind map of or list the different consequences that might occur if students did one of the above. Note that there are different consequences. Ask students to be aware of the choices they can make.

Share with students that when we express emotion, we are setting emotional energy in motion and we can expect a reaction. Ask students to explore what happens if they greet someone with great emotional joy. What happens if they greet someone angrily? If they cry when they see a friend?

Next, ask students to write a short story about the consequences of greeting someone in these three ways. Compare stories. Does our attitude have an effect, or consequence, on our relationship with someone else?

# Flying Further

The following are related activities that you can use in history, geography, and literature.

* ★ Read a story almost to the end but stop right before the end. Now ask the students to make up their own ending.

* ★ Ask students what life would be like today if something different had happened in history. What if Columbus had not landed in the Americas? What if Joan of Arc had not been burned? What if Harriet Tubman had not escaped from slavery? What if President Lincoln had not been shot? What if Pearl Harbor had not been bombed? Have students rewrite history in a historical report, a news release, or a newscast.

* ★ What if lions lived in New York City? Palm trees grew in northern countries? Chickens were ten feet tall? Students can make up their own what ifs, draw pictures of the consequences, write a short report, or find their own way to express a geographical what if.

* ★ Ask students to choose an aspect of the class schedule or physical structure that feels like a problem. Have the students brainstorm as many different solutions as they can. What if we . . . ? Explain to students that in brainstorming it is okay to be silly, to think of wild answers. A wonderful idea might emerge from one of these silly thoughts.

# CHAPTER THREE

# The Journey: Life as a Process

*The future belongs to those who believe in their dreams.*
—Eleanor Roosevelt

*The growth of the human mind is still high adventure, in many ways the highest adventure on earth.*
—Norman Cousins

*I desire that there be as many different persons in the world as possible; I would have each one be very careful to find out and preserve his [or her] own way.*
—Henry David Thoreau

When we come into the world and take our first breath, we have also made our first independent step on the journey through life. We have become travelers and our journey will lead us into difficult times and through wonderful places. We will be forever moving, constantly making new discoveries and finding fresh challenges.

Life will present us with many varied experiences and throughout life we will create a personal vision of our journey that will determine how we meet each challenge. Some people find life's journey fascinating; others are frightened or angered by life's events. While some people face tough trials and continuously rise to the challenge, others become discouraged with life's difficulties. What is the difference between the two? Attitude. Our attitude will determine whether we view rocks on our path as boulders to struggle around or opportunities that may hold gems inside a rough and dirty exterior.

For the people who recognize that cycles of positive and negative experiences are a natural occurrence in life, the journey will flow through difficult times. For people whose goal in life is to discover a plateau of peace with unvarying regularity, life may become a nightmare of disappointments.

Perhaps one of the greatest duties we have as mentors for our children is to help them develop attitudes that will help them face life's challenges with courage and insight. This chapter contains activities to help students form positive life attitudes by understanding the processes, experiences, and visions in life's journey.

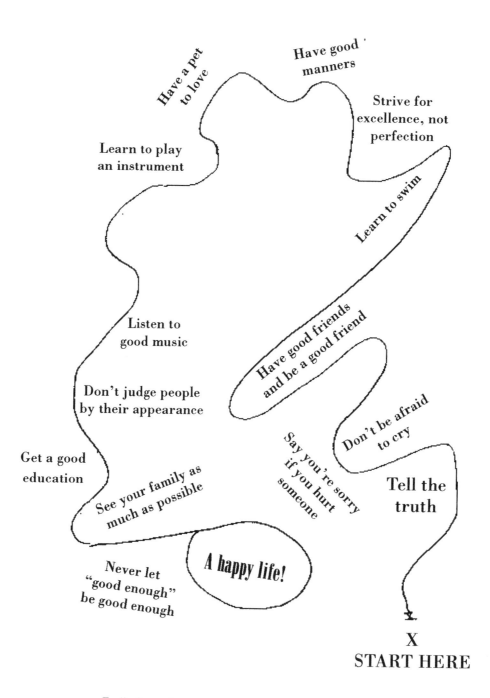

Have a pet to love

Have good manners

Strive for excellence, not perfection

Learn to play an instrument

Learn to swim

Listen to good music

Have good friends and be a good friend

Don't judge people by their appearance

Don't be afraid to cry

Say you're sorry if you hurt someone

Tell the truth

Get a good education

See your family as much as possible

A happy life!

Never let "good enough" be good enough

X
**START HERE**

Emily Cummings

# Life Processes

The Latin word *processus* means "to proceed and go forward." Life is a processus, a moving forward through repeated experiences of growing, learning, knowing, sharing. When we recognize that we are in the midst of a life process, moving through the difficult parts of the process seems less intimidating. Just as we often make the journey up a steep hill with stronger strides when we can see the top of the hill, we may make the journey through difficult times more easily if we can see an end to the difficulties.

Understanding life's processes will help all of us to accept responsibility for moving forward through life's challenges with creative action and intention. In the following activities students have opportunities to recognize and understand life processes.

# 60 Beginnings

All things have a beginning and an ending. Beginnings can be important road marks in our lives. When we recognize a beginning we feel the excitement of starting something new, appreciate the initiation of an idea, and honor the birth of a creation. While some firsts are part of natural processes for which we can claim no credit, other firsts are personal creations that we initiate.

In our society, we have come to think of creativity as an artistic talent that only a few people possess. But the *process* of creation is something we all do. We are constantly creating, whether the result is a picture or a musical song, a new friendship or a new role in life, a better way of walking to school or a new way to fix our hair. Living life is an act of creation and being creative in *how* we live our lives can make the journey more interesting and easier!

This activity gives students a sense of how many beginnings there are in life and helps them realize the many ways they create. Remembering past firsts will help young students develop the concept of beginnings. You can share these firsts as a way to get to know one another better.

## Activity

Let students know that they will be creating a Book of Firsts that will record all their "first" experiences. Every time they do something for the first time, they will begin a new page entitled "My First . . ." Explain that firsts can occur in any area of life. For example, My First

- ★ "A" on a spelling test
- ★ time to have my new friend over to my house
- ★ male teacher
- ★ flute lesson
- ★ picture drawn with oil pastels

- ★ chance to help Mom build something in her workshop

- ★ chance to help Dad bake cookies

- ★ experience making dinner by myself

- ★ pair of hiking boots

Students go through their Book of Firsts periodically and write down what other experiences occurred that were related to their firsts. They may be able to write that now they get A's in spelling all the time, that the new friend is a regular visitor to their home, that they have decided they like having a male teacher. Some firsts may have already ended; perhaps the student has quit flute lessons or grown out of the hiking boots. Whatever has occurred, students will benefit from recognizing how many changes and opportunities they have in their lives. I hope they will have experiences that illustrate that their actions and attitudes make a difference in how their experiences turn out.

You may want students to begin this activity by making a list of past firsts in their lives. Following are some suggestions:

- ★ first tooth

- ★ first bicycle

- ★ first day of school

> Children are born passionately eager to make as much sense as they can of things around them.
>
> —John Holt

# 61 Buds and Butterflies

Lindsey Dombroski

Children and teenagers grow and change rapidly. The processes of growth and transformation are elements of every stage of life but are perhaps the most dramatic in childhood.

Nature holds wonderful examples of transformation and growth for us in two of its most lovely life forms: flowers and butterflies. Even young children can understand growth and transformation processes by exploring them in flowers and butterflies. Following is a collection of activities that will help students recognize growth and transformation in themselves and in nature.

## Activities

Have students find a position in which they feel like a seed planted in the ground. Play imagery music and ask the students to mime the action of growing into a flower.

Have the students draw large individual circles on pieces of paper. The circles are seeds that represent the children. Ask the children to draw "sprouts" coming out of their seeds and to label the sprouts according to what has happened to them so far. Then ask them to draw pictures inside the seeds of everything they think will be in their future.

Explain to your students that sometimes we are like the creature inside the cocoon, wrapped in our own comfortable world and waiting for the right moment to emerge. At other times we may be like the butterfly flitting from place to place. Have them write a short paragraph or two based on the sentence, "When I am . . . I would like to be in a cocoon." Then have them write about the times they feel like flying and exploring like a butterfly.

Have students make a cocoon from a large box or blankets. Let them go into the cocoon for a few moments when they are feeling as if they need time alone. Tell them that when they come out they will feel "transformed" and ready to be butterflies in the world.

The following activities were designed by Caron B. Goode and Joy Lehni Watson (1992).

★ Ask students to discuss or brainstorm answers to this question: How is being a seed that grows into a flower like being a child growing up?

★ Have students choose objects in nature that represent them best. For example, a student may feel sturdy like a rock, happy like a daisy, pretty like a tulip, or easygoing like a breeze. Ask students to draw pictures of their nature symbols and explain the symbols. Display the pictures on a bulletin board.

★ Have students each plant a seed, water it, and watch it grow under their care.

★ Ask students to draw the flowering process, beginning with the seed and progressing through the development of a stem and leaves, a bud, and then a flower. Students can label parts or discuss the steps.

★ Read the book *Monty the Butterfly* or other children's books about butterflies to the class and discuss the transformation a caterpillar makes into a butterfly.

★ Lead students through a guided imagery of being inside a cocoon and emerging as a butterfly to explore the world. (Caron and Joy have a wonderful guided imagery, "My Butterfly Emerges," in their book.) After the experience, ask students these questions: What did it feel like to be inside a cocoon? What is the first thing you remember about breaking through the cocoon? Did you see anything special when you went exploring as a butterfly?

★ Ask the children to draw or paint the butterflies they can imagine themselves to be.

★ Have the children write short poems, choosing one of the following titles or making up their own: "I Fly Like the Butterfly," "A Butterfly Is Free," "From a Caterpillar to a Butterfly."

★ Study the stages from caterpillar to butterfly and discuss how each stage is like a part of growing up.

# 62 Changing Images

We constantly change throughout life. Our bodies grow, develop, and deteriorate. Though we have physical features that remain constant throughout our lives, sometimes we can hardly believe that the person whose face is reflected in the mirror each morning is the same person as the two-year-old with the identical name that we have seen in photographs. The two-year-old and the older person appear to be different individuals because their abilities, goals, and activities are not similar.

During each stage of life there are tasks, learning experiences, and roles that are unique aspects of that part of life's journey. Although everyone recognizes that there are differences between the stages of adolescence, youth, adulthood, parenthood, different careers, and the golden years, some societies have lost track of the ceremonies and rituals that have historically been performed to mark passage from one stage into another. An official rite of passage into a new life phase is an important statement that allows people to acknowledge the changes that will occur as they accept new responsibilities, create new patterns of living, and realize new opportunities.

Children need to have a solid comprehension of the nature and number of opportunities inherent in future stages so the children can prepare to meet the needs of the next life stage. The current flood of books on the market about various life stages, begun by Gail Sheehan's *Passages,* is a testimony to the interest and concerns our society has with knowing what to expect as our roles change.

Here is an activity to help students learn more about life's stages and to allow them to recognize how far they have come on their journey. Combine this activity with Wearing Hats from chapter 1 for more insight into life roles.

## Activity

Ask students to bring photographs of themselves at three different ages between infancy and their current age. Have them review the pictures and note similarities and differences in their bodies. Next, have them write short descriptions of themselves that reflect how they remember feeling at each age. Have them also write what they feel they have learned and accomplished during each of the life stages they have completed so far. What do they feel are the goals and lessons of their current life stage?

Show students books or illustrations of people in various life stages and especially at these passage points:

**birth**
**infancy**
**toddlerhood**
**elementary school years**
**early teen years**
**high school graduation**
**college or career-building years**
**weddings**
**parenthood**
**mid-life**
**retirement transitions**
**golden years**
**death**

Ask students to create a visual collage, time line, or mural of the various life stages. Students may want to draw, use clay for sculptures, or cut pictures out of magazines for their artwork. Suggest that they include symbols representing the key goals, lessons, and opportunities for each stage. Ask them to title their work.

Display the students' pictures and descriptions or have students make a special folder about themselves and put the portraits in the folder. This project is good for getting to know one another better.

# Flying Further

The following are related activities that you can use in art and health.

★ Find a book showing some of Vincent Van Gogh's self-portraits and have students compare the different views Van Gogh had of himself in his more than forty self-portraits. Have students research Van Gogh's deteriorating mental state and note how it affected his portraits.

★ Find pictures of people at various ages and study the growth, development, and change in the body over a lifetime. Relate this to current health issues. What changes are there in mental growth?

# 63 Ups and Downs

Bobbi Jacobsen

Life is full of ups and downs. We can gain an interesting perspective of our lives when we chart our past experiences and note how we felt as we were going through them. If we look carefully at past experiences that seem negative, we will often find that there were positive aspects that helped us to learn more about life.

## Activity

Ask students to take three or four minutes to sit quietly and think about two positive experiences from their past. Ask them to remember two negative experiences. Next, ask them to use a marker to draw a line on a piece of paper. They will draw the positive experiences as peaks and the negative experiences as valleys.

Ask the students to draw symbols or write titles for the positive experiences. Have them do the same for the negative experiences. Have students share their experiences with a partner, if they choose.

Next, have students turn the drawings upside down so the peaks become valleys and the valleys become peaks. Ask them to reflect on the new peaks. Was there something good that happened as a result of the experience? In what ways did they grow and learn from the experience? Have them share their thoughts with a friend. They might also reflect on whether or not the experiences they viewed as positive peaks were possibly negative valleys for someone else.

# Flying Further

The following are related activities that you can use in science, history, and language arts.

★ Have students interview an older person in the community and ask that person to describe one of the worst things that happened to him or her that later turned out to have positive effects. Have students write a short story based on the interview or share what they found out with the class.

★ Ask students to consider a negative situation in their lives. Can they think of any positive results that may arise from it? Is there anything they might do that could create a positive result?

★ Ask students to find an event in the current history lesson that appeared to be negative at the time it occurred. Now have students explore the events that followed. In what ways did the event result in positive changes? See if students can find an example of an event that seemed to be positive when it occurred but later proved to have negative effects.

★ Discuss natural cycles such as human and animal life and death, geologic building and weathering processes, photosynthesis and respiration, or evaporation and condensation. In what ways does everything in life grow and change? How can this change be related to the human life experience? What can we learn from observing natural cycles?

# 64 Life Discovery Maps

Emily Cummings

Here is an extension of the Ups and Downs activity that helps students to see life as a journey.

## Activity

Have students draw a picture of a road on a large piece of paper to represent their personal Life Discovery Map. Ask them to think of four highlights in their lives and draw four road signs along their roads to mark these highlights. Have the students write two or three words or draw a symbol inside each sign to represent one of the highlights. Next, ask students to close their eyes and reflect upon their future. Ask them to think of four goals they would like to complete. Have them make a Future Life Map by drawing another road and placing future goals in the signposts.

Allow each student to share her or his Discovery and Future Life Map with a friend. Ask students to explain the signposts along their journey and to share their hopes for the future. Save the maps. In a few months, ask students to review their maps and see if they would like to make changes. If so, allow them time to draw new Future Life Maps.

## Flying Further

The following are related activities that you can use in history, science, and language arts.

★ Use the Discovery Map idea to have students outline a historical event that you are studying. Students can display on signposts four points of the event they feel were important. They can make additional drawings on the map to depict other aspects of the historical event. Students can use the maps as study guides.

★ Have students make a Discovery Map that shows the important "signposts" or steps within a science cycle. Have them draw illustrations on or around the signs to define the cycle further.

★ Ask students to make a Discovery Map of main events from a book or story in their current reading assignment.

★ Many people feel more comfortable in a classroom when they know what to expect during the day or in a particular lesson. New information may also have more relevance when we can see how it fits into the total picture. A road map that highlights the important steps in a lesson plan provides students with an understanding of the learning process and encourages them to recognize the importance of personal responsibility in learning. Some of your students will appreciate your using symbols and pictures rather than words in an outline.

Choose a particular unit and outline the four to six most important signposts along the discovery journey. Using colored chalk on a chalkboard or colored markers on a large sheet of drawing paper or flip chart, give the road map a title. Draw a road, label one end start and the other end finish, and label signposts with your main points along the road. You may want to decorate the roadway with trees, buildings, streams, or whatever feels appropriate. Explain to your students that they will follow the road map on the discovery journey. Refer to the map periodically as you travel through the lessons, or keep track of your progress by coloring in the road as you progress. You can use a road map to outline the flow of a day as well.

May Brewer

# 65 Tracking Your Discoveries

Making a new discovery can be an exciting and rewarding experience. When we take the time to honor a discovery, we develop a sense of accomplishment and a feeling of moving forward in our learning. By naming a learning discovery, we make the discovery more important and we will remember the information more easily later. A visual chart of discoveries can give students and teachers a sense of a student's learning process and may reveal areas in which students need more help.

## Activity

At the beginning of a week, give each student five copies of the discovery chart that follows. (The chart is also included in the appendix.) You may want to have students use construction paper to create discovery folders to hold their charts. At the end of each lesson, ask students to review what they learned in the lesson and think about the discoveries they made. Give them a minute or two to write their most important discoveries on their charts. They can write on the charts while you prepare the next lesson. You may have students review their discoveries by themselves at the end of the day or share the discoveries with a partner. You may also have them review at the end of the week.

Do this activity for at least one week. (For older students, you will want to design your own chart with the appropriate subjects.) When students are familiar with keeping track of their discoveries, have them make a discovery chart that tracks personal discoveries. Students can keep track of what they learned about themselves, about a friend, about friendship, about conflict resolution, about working with other people, or about any project in self-worth or personal development.

# My Discoveries

Name _____Date _____

Today I made these discoveries:

Reading


Spelling


Language Arts


History, Social Studies


Science


Math


Music, Art


P.E., Health

# 66 Endings

Life is a series of endings. An ending may be an accomplishment, such as completing Brownies and moving to Girl Scouts. An ending often brings mixed emotions, such as when the school year ends and students are proud of their accomplishment, sad to leave their teacher, and excited about the summer. An ending might also represent a permanent end to a relationship, such as through death or relocation. This kind of ending may trigger the grief process.

Loss and the ensuing grief are a part of life that few of us enjoy but at some point we all experience. Elizabeth Kübler-Ross has helped us realize that there is a normal emotional process we move through when we grieve. This emotional process occurs whenever we lose anything we value. When I lost my wallet, I went through a grief process that was simply a smaller version of an intense grieving process I went through following the death of my business partner and dear friend of twelve years (to whom this book is dedicated).

The grief process includes many emotions. Denial, anger, grief, and acceptance are all part of the recurring cycle that we experience as we learn to adjust to our loss. Often people alternate between feeling hope and feeling despair. While the grief over the loss of a wallet may last a day or two, the grieving process for a loved one may last years, though there are adjustments over time.

Children's concept of death is different from adults'. Very young children may ask when Grandpa is coming back even though they have been told he is dead. One college student told me that even months after her father's death, her young daughter continued to mention that Grandpa had promised her an ice cream cone, as if she expected him to return and fulfill his promise.

Sometimes children think they are in some way responsible for a loss. Studies have shown that children go through a grief process when their parents divorce and that the children often feel responsible in some way for the divorce, even though a parent may reassure them it is not their fault. Children also often feel that they are responsible for a loved one's death.

The Endings activities provide an opportunity to teach children how to recognize and honor endings and to deal more effectively with grief and the loss of objects, pets, and people.

# Activities

Discuss with students that life is full of changes and a change may mean the end of something old as well as the beginning of something new. As Picasso once said, "Every act of con-struction is first an act of de-struction." Beginnings and endings go hand in hand. Children cannot go on to fifth grade without finishing fourth grade. While becoming a fifth-grade student may be exciting, it does mean the end of fourth grade, and this change may make a student sad as well as joyful.

If students have a Book of Firsts from the Beginnings activity, they can use this book to help them learn about endings. Work with your students to develop a way to honor endings. An ending, though perhaps sad, will at least feel complete if there is a feeling of closure, if the ending is noted and honored. Here are some closure ideas:

★ If a beginning that was noted in a student's Book of Firsts is now ending, suggest that the student write the rest of his or her experience in the Book of Firsts. The student can write about how the event developed, how it ended, what was enjoyable, what wasn't enjoyable, and what the student felt he or she learned from the experience. Finalizing the ending with a few words that summarize the experience and point out both positive and negative aspects of the experience will help the student to feel closure.

★ If students do not have a Book of Firsts, you can have them write or share orally the story of an ending experience. Students can do this exercise to help them feel closure after the loss of a special item as well as the loss of a relationship. Students can explain where they got the special item, how they used it, and, if they can replace it, whether or not they would get the same item or a different one. They may want to share what special meaning the item held for them.

★ Have students make a list or mind map of all the negative and positive aspects of an experience that has ended. Then ask them to make a list or mind map of the positive and negative aspects of the ending itself. A discussion about these lists is important. Remember that the idea is not to make the change "okay" or deny negative or sad feelings, but simply to recognize, honor, and learn from the experience.

★ Have students write something they would *like* to get rid of on a slip of paper. They will usually write down a bad habit or a negative feeling. The students put their papers into a large coffee can or some other metal container. Drop a lit match into the container as students stand witness while their papers burn and the unwanted thoughts go up in smoke. Students can write or share new beginnings or habits they will replace the negative thoughts with.

# Life Experiences

Brandi Owen

Each of us has unique life experiences that are shaped by our surroundings, beliefs, and attitudes. Our past experiences will influence how we make decisions and determine how we address future goals. As children we may believe that everyone has experiences similar to ours. Indeed, we all face some of the same aspects of life, but many life experiences are unique. When we tell others of our life experiences and learn about the experiences of others, we glimpse the depth and breadth of life. Some of the stories students share with us may open our eyes to the variety of opportunities available in life, while other stories may make us feel blessed for the ease of our journey and feel compassion for the rugged journeys of other people.

The process of reviewing past personal experiences can help us recognize patterns in our lives and uncover great moments of learning. As we review our present experiences we can see developing trends that shape our lives. We can use these insights to help us make decisions about how we choose to direct our lives in the future. The activities in this section will give students opportunities to recognize the variety of experiences that are part of life's journey and help them gain new perspectives about the direction of their lives.

# 67 Life Drawings

This activity reviews life experiences through the "scape" drawing concept used in Energy Cycle Circles and Soundscapes. I have done this activity successfully with people of all ages, including older adults living in extended care units. Because the art is abstract and must be explained, wonderful stories emerge as people share the meaning of their scapes. Be sure to leave plenty of sharing time for stories to emerge. This is a good getting-to-know-others activity.

## Activity

In this activity, students make three scape drawings to represent three different times in their lives. Suggest three appropriate ages for students to focus on, such as preschool years, elementary school years, and early teen years. The ages you select will depend to a great deal on the age of your students. Explain to students that they will be making drawings to reflect their feelings and experiences during each of the ages. They will use lines, shapes, and colors in their drawings, but no symbols.

Ask students to draw three circles, one for each age scape. The circles may all be on one paper or each on a separate paper. Ask students to label each circle with one of the ages you have given them. Give the students five minutes to draw in each circle. Post the pictures on a bulletin board so students can see each other's Life Drawings.

> The secret of education lies in respecting the pupil.
> —Ralph Waldo Emerson

# 68 Talking Circle

Every person has unique experiences in life. We can learn from each other by sharing some of these experiences. In the process of hearing others' life stories, students have a chance to hear about experiences that may be different from their own. The use of the talking stick helps students develop listening skills and patience. They will also learn that listening quietly is a way to show someone respect.

Do this activity once each week for twenty to thirty minutes. You may want to have each student share for two or three minutes, or have five students share for five or six minutes each week. Consider using a timer to keep students' sharing to the desired time. Students in sixth grade and up can usually share in a smaller circle of six to ten students once they have done the activity a few times and understand the process. Younger students may always need to sit in one large group unless you have adult helpers.

You will find that this time becomes very special to students and will greatly increase student bonding and self-worth.

## Activity

Find an object in the classroom to use as a talking stick. The object may be a stick to which you have added decorations (beads, string, yarn, feathers, and so on), or it may be a stone or other object. Explain to the students that they are going to share in a talking circle. Each student will have an opportunity to share but can choose not to share, as well. Show the students the talking stick and explain that only the person with the talking stick can speak. Everyone else must be very quiet and not speak at all. Explain that the talking circle will be used to share life stories— important parts of each student's past. Each week you can ask students to share about a specific aspect of their lives. Because of the number of students in most classrooms, students should keep their stories to two minutes unless you have decided to spend more time on a specific question.

Following are some suggestions of questions and discussion points to use in the talking circle:

★ Where were you born and what is the first thing you remember?

★ Where did your mother, father, foster parent, or other adult important in your life grow up and where is this person's family originally from?

★ How many brothers and sisters do you have and how old are they? Share what you think is special about each one.

★ What is one of your family traditions?

★ Share something you enjoy very much about your family.

★ What would you like to do with your family that you have not done before?

★ What do your parents do for a living? If you have gone to work with one of them, share what you experienced there.

★ Share a story you remember about one of your relatives.

★ Remember back to a particularly good experience you have had and share what it was.

★ Share an accomplishment that you are particularly proud of.

★ Share something that you would love to do if you could do anything you wanted to do.

★ Share something about an animal that has been a family pet or one you have seen somewhere.

You may want to ask students to design questions for the talking circle.

# Flying Further

★ Use the talking circle at the end of the day for a ten-minute review of the day's learning experiences. Have each student share one thing that was particularly meaningful or interesting that she or he learned during the day.

★ Give students special time to do independent research at the library, learning center, or through required readings. At the end of the research time, meet in the circle and have each student share one fact or concept discovered in the research.

# **69** Daily Events

William Wildanger

The habits and routines we include in the structures of our days will determine our life experiences to some degree. Our daily patterns dictate how much free time we have, the direction of our energy, and what activities we incorporate into our lives. Daily routines also have a great effect on how we feel. When we do too many things we may feel rushed. If we don't allow time to eat correctly, we may be hungry or uncomfortable. If we don't have quiet time, we may become grouchy.

Some parts of our daily routine may have been set for us by someone else, but there are many aspects of even a second-grader's day that she or he can change. Sometimes we continue a habit without realizing that we have other options. We may feel we can't do something we'd like to do because we don't think we have enough time. We may not realize that we could change our daily routines to make time. Children need to know that their habits and routines become their life experiences and that they can take responsibility for what they would like their lives to be. This activity offers students an opportunity to review their daily habits and routines, to recognize that they can adjust their daily patterns, and to establish priorities for their time.

## Activity

Ask students to list six events that occur daily or more than once a week in their lives. Ask younger students to think of four. Have students select four of these events and draw pictures to illustrate their selections. When the drawings are complete, have students share descriptions of the events.

Next, ask the students to think of two things they would like to have in their lives that they could incorporate into their daily routines and how they might include these activities in their daily routines. What does including the activities require? When and how would students do the activities? Have students draw pictures of what they would look like doing these activities. Suggest that students pick one of their activities and add it to their daily routine during the next two weeks. At the end of two weeks, have them evaluate whether or not they liked their lives better with this change. If so, how did the activity add to their lives? If not, why not?

# Flying Further

The following are related activities that you can use in creative writing, art, history, and social studies.

* ★ Have the students use the pictures as a stimulus for writing a creative story about their lives or a particular event in their lives. Students can also trade pictures and write a story about someone else's pictures.
* ★ Ask students to select a person from history and find out about his or her life. Students can draw four pictures about the person's daily life or specific events that occurred in his or her life.
* ★ Ask students to research the lifestyle of another culture and draw four daily events pictures that reflect what life is like for a child in that culture.
* ★ Ask students to explore the paintings of artists, such as Norman Rockwell and Mary Cassatt, who drew about the daily events in people's lives. Have the students select one or two favorites and share reproductions of them with the class.

# **70** **Walk in My Shoes**

Sarah Cook

Here is a wonderful activity for broadening students' perspectives about life and the life experiences of others. This activity is a good way for people to get to know one another, and it works for young and old people alike.

## Activity

Ask students to write a short description of their daily lives. Have them include what happens on a normal school day before and after school. They can also include two things they feel are benefits in their life and two things they think are hard about their lives. Share with your students that everyone's life journey is different and that sometimes we don't realize just how different people's lives are until we have "walked in" another person's shoes, or imagined what it would be like to live another person's life.

Have the students sit together in one large circle. Ask them to take their shoes off and place their shoes and life descriptions in front of them. Everyone stands and begins to walk clockwise around the circle. Play the song "Walk a Mile in My Shoes" by Joe South or introspective piano music. When students have walked around the circle and are not by their own shoes, ask the group to stop or signal them to stop by stopping the music. In front of them will be someone else's shoes and life description. Ask the students to read the other person's life description. Have the students put their own shoes back on, and, if possible, take the students for a walk around the playground. Ask them not to talk but to think about what it would be like to be the person whose life description they read.

When you return to the classroom, ask the students to write or share how it felt to imagine being this other person. What would they like about being this other person? What wouldn't they like? How is the other person's life different from theirs? How is it similar? How does knowing what another person's life is like make them feel about the lives they lead?

# Flying Further

The following are related activities that you can use in history, social studies, language arts, and art.

★ Write six daily life descriptions for your students based on the lives of children from around the world, or have your students read the stories and write the daily life experiences. You can use such stories as "The Story of Little Tree" to get accurate information about children's lives. Repeat the circling activity described in step 6. Students need not take off their shoes. Have the students each read the description they receive and imagine what their lives would be like if they were walking in the shoes of the child whose life they read about. At the end of the day ask students to share or write what this experience was like for them.

★ Use life descriptions based on current events and social studies. For example, have each student research what the daily life of a child would be like if that child were one of the following:

a child starving in Somalia

a child living in Micronesia

a child living in Romania after the Timosoar
    a revolution

a child living in the inner city in America

a child living on a ranch in Montana

an Inuit child living in Alaska

a child who has won an Olympic gold medal

**a child who works all day in the rice paddies of Asia**

**a child living in Vietnam today**

**a child whose parent is a politician**

★ Students can trade descriptions and "walk in the shoes" of different children each day for a week, sharing their experiences with one another.

★ Have students research and write life descriptions about children from different eras of history. Following are some suggestions: an enslaved African in the South during the Civil War, a Taino Indian that Columbus "discovered," a pioneer who traveled across the United States in a covered wagon, a person who experienced the French Revolution, a person who survived the Plague in Europe, or a Jew in Eastern Europe during World War II. Students can trade descriptions and share experiences with one another, journal about their feelings, or report to the class.

★ After students have walked in the shoes of another person, have each of them make a drawing or picture collage that illustrates the lives they experienced and their feelings about walking in someone else's shoes.

# 71 Life Is Like a . . .

Metaphors are a powerful learning tool because they give meaning to information and people remember them more easily than mere facts. This activity gives students a chance to develop a metaphor that reflects their personal feelings and attitudes about life.

## Activity

Explain to your students that a metaphor is a figure of speech that suggests a likeness between two things. You can explore such metaphors as "He was as grouchy as a bear"; "The bed was as hard as a rock"; "The ship plowed through the sea." Show a picture of an object and ask the students to think of the ways that they feel life is like the object. Following are some examples:

★ Life is like a race car because . . . it moves so fast!
★ Life is like an old tennis shoe because . . . it's so comfortable!

Give students time to browse through magazines and find pictures that reflect their feelings about life or give the students pictures to choose from. Students glue the pictures to a piece of drawing paper and complete the sentence "Life Is Like a . . . " by writing metaphors by their pictures. Let students explain their metaphors to partners and display the metaphor pictures on a wall.

> The principal goal of education is to create people who are capable of doing new things, not simply of repeating what other generations have done—people who are creative, inventive, and discoverers. The second goal of education is to form minds which can be critical, can verify, and not accept everything they are offered.
>
> —Jean Piaget

164

# 72 Learning Circle

This activity uses the circle drawing technique to provide students and teachers with insight into students' attitudes about learning. This activity is good to do at the beginning of the year and repeat at the end of the year. Save the first drawings and compare them to the second ones to see if there are any changes.

## Activity

Have the students draw large circles on pieces of paper. Ask them to close their eyes and imagine the colors and shapes of their feelings while you ask them the following questions and give them the following directions:

★ How do you feel about your learning experiences?
★ Imagine the learning subjects you like best.
★ Imagine the learning subjects you like least.
★ What colors and shapes illustrate your feelings about learning?

When students have had a moment to image, ask them to draw lines, shapes, and colors in their learning circles to illustrate their images. Allow them several minutes to complete the drawings. Ask students to share their drawings.

> Researches I have conducted show that a person will permit himself to be known when he believes his audience is a man of goodwill.
>
> —Sidney M. Jourard

# 73 Mapping Our Home

Phil Gang (1992), once a Montessori teacher, recognized the need for hands-on ecology tools and designed manipulatable curriculum materials called *Our Planet, Our Home.* I had the good fortune to work with Phil when he rewrote the teacher's guide to include holistic activities. One of the activities we designed helps students understand how Earth provides for the needs of all life forms in much the same way that our personal homes provide for our family's needs.

Following is a similar activity that helps students realize and appreciate the systems necessary in a home as well as the Earth systems necessary for survival. This activity also gives students a sense of their need to participate in personal home and Earth home maintenance.

## Activity

As a class, mind map the various parts of a home. Begin by writing the word *home* in the center of a circle on a chalkboard. Ask students to think about what is in their homes and have them share their thoughts with the group. Write students' ideas on the mind map or draw simple symbols to represent the various elements. As students share their ideas, categorize the ideas into the topics shown in the Home and Needs list that follows. (The list is also included in the appendix.)

Ask students to help you make a mind map of the elements of our larger home, planet Earth. Place the word *Earth* at the center of the mind map, and as students make suggestions for the mind map, categorize their responses into the same Home and Needs categories.

When you have completed the two mind maps, have students compare the elements of their personal home with the elements of our planetary home. Discuss the similarities of human needs in our two homes.

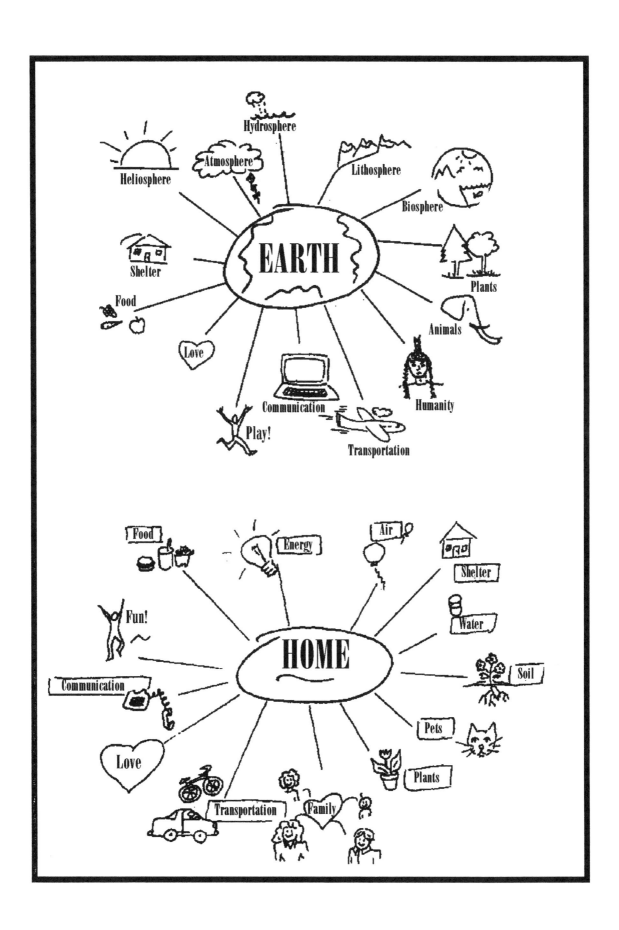

## Home and Needs

The following list of Earth/home systems and human needs can be used to direct and categorize students' ideas during the mind mapping.

| Earth/Home Systems | Human Needs |
|---|---|
| Air: Atmosphere | Shelter |
| Land: Lithosphere | Food |
| Water: Hydrosphere | Transportation |
| Energy: Heliosphere | Communication |
| Plants, Animals, Living Things: Biosphere | Recreation |
| | Love |

# Flying Further

The following are related activities that you can use in science, ecology, history, and social studies.

★ Have students research the five Earth systems: heliosphere, atmosphere, hydrosphere, lithosphere, and biosphere. How does each of these systems contribute to the functioning of Earth as a home system for Earth creatures?

★ Have students find out how different cultures meet their members' basic needs. How do different cultures relate to the various Earth systems? Have the students make a mind map of how another culture meets its members' needs: What kind of transportation does the culture use? What role do animals play in daily life? What form of communication do they use? What kind of shelter do they have? What do they take from Earth and how do they care for Earth? Discuss the mind maps.

★ Ask students to make a mind map of how people met their needs one hundred, two hundred, five hundred, or two thousand years ago. How do the mind maps compare? Discuss how human needs and lifestyles have changed. What has created the changes? What do students imagine our needs will be one hundred years from now?

★ One of the activities in *Our Planet, Our Home* is a powerful lesson that helps people recognize just how much we depend on Earth systems. Begin erasing elements one by one from the HOME mind map, and as you erase each one, ask students if humans could survive without that element. Which elements would students miss the most? Which ones would be impossible to live without? Do the same for the mind map of EARTH. At the very end, erase humans from the picture. Would Earth systems still function without humans? In reality, while Earth systems couldn't function without air, land, the sun, or water, the absence of people would not alter the successful functioning of these systems. Have students reflect on the meaning of this revelation. Discuss what we might need to do to keep Earth systems intact.

# Life Visions

Whether we recognize it or not, we each hold a vision of our future. Our goals may be clearly set or we may simply live day to day with little expectation or sense of responsibility for the outcome of each day. We may seek to accomplish many things in our lives or we may hope only for an uneventful day. Whatever our vision is, our goals and desires will lead us to choose which paths to take in the forks in the roads before us.

When we have a model or a picture of the future we desire, we can make conscious choices that lead to making our desired future a reality. In the Life Visions activities students can explore future possibilities and find ways to create a vision of the pathways that will lead them to their goals. When we can envision our future, we can find the road that leads to it.

# 74 Stretching Yourself

Each person's success in the classroom and in life is greatly determined by his or her self-perception. When we learn to expand the boundaries of self-perception within our own minds, we may be able to expand them in reality. The use of clay and the kinesthetic body movements in this activity help to create a strong internal image of stretching to greater heights.

## Activity

Tell your students they are going to stretch themselves in mind and body. Begin by having students work clay in their hands until it is soft. I use polyform clay because it is easy to use and store. When the clay is soft, ask students to see how many ways they can stretch it. They should experiment with making it longer, taller, wider, fatter, and with pulling it into peaks. Have them work with the clay for four or five minutes.

Ask your students to stand and close their eyes. Have them imagine being firmly connected to the ground. Play stretching music and tell students to reach as high into the air as they can, standing on their tiptoes. Now ask students to reach down and touch the floor, then stretch as far as they can to each side. See how far they can reach behind them. Let them explore their space by reaching as far as they can in as many directions as possible. To help your students, suggest that they imagine stretching in the same ways that they stretched their clay.

Ask students to stop moving and, with their eyes closed, imagine their bodies reaching as far as they can in all directions. Ask your students each to envision a goal they would like to accomplish. Tell them to imagine quietly themselves reaching toward their goal until they have attained it. Ask them to see themselves going through the steps to reach it and then to imagine themselves actually doing it. Let them enjoy and experience this vision for two or three minutes.

# 75 Inspiration

Chris Atkinson

Martin Luther King, Jr., once said, "I have a dream . . . ," inspired many others to find their own dreams, and got help that would contribute to making his dream a reality. Having a dream is a strong motivational element that leads toward accomplishing a goal.

This guided imagery was written by Caron B. Goode and Joy Lehni Watson (1992). The story emphasizes dreaming and helps students imagine higher achievement. Inspiration is symbolized by an eagle soaring to higher perspectives and coming to rest on a mountaintop, the symbolic pinnacle of higher goals.

Caron and Joy suggest that you adapt this guided imagery by changing the story line or the dream or goal to help your students reach their goals in specific subjects, such as creative writing, speech-making, or personal motivation. Once students have had help practicing goal-setting, they can begin to make goal-setting an integral part of their lives.

# Activity

Ask students to sit or lie comfortably with their eyes closed. Play relax-ation or imagery music, and after giving students one minute to relax, read the following imagery:

*Imagine the mighty eagle with long, broad wings and powerful, hooked bill and strong talons. It sits watching you, waiting for you to climb upon its expansive wings to fly with it over desert terrain. Do so now. When you have settled upon the eagle's back and are ready for flight, signal me by raising your hand slightly.* (Pause and wait for the majority of the students to signal you before moving ahead.)

*The glorious eagle flaps its huge wings, lifting gently upward. Higher . . . higher . . . and higher still.* (Pause for a moment.)

*Look at the expansive sky before you—light blue extending across the wide horizon. Feel the moist texture of the puffy clouds as the eagle takes you higher on its back.*

*Now look below you at the desert: the endless dunes of rolling sand . . . the tapestry of dusty brown and deep green . . . and shadowed rivulets of ancient river beds, long ago dried up. Occasionally, you can see patches of tall trees reaching their spindly arms toward you.*

*Feel the exhilaration of the swift movement as you ride on the eagle. Your spirit flies free. What do you dream in this freedom? What inspires you as you move steadily toward the majestic mountains in the distance? The wind whips through your hair. The bird dips and circles. Hang on! I'll be silent for a moment while you experience the feeling of flying, the feeling of inspiration!* (Pause, giving students a couple of moments to anchor the feeling.)

*The eagle begins its descent, soaring and circling downward now, toward a cinnamon-colored moun-tain below you. Ride those bumpy wind currents as you watch the rocky outcropping on the mountain top grow closer. The eagle cranes its neck forward. Its wings pull up and back, like a parachute, break-ing the momentum of flight. The eagle stretches its legs forward for balance and extends its talons. Gently it descends, and you roll off onto a patch of soft, sandy earth. Look around you as you stand on top of the mountain, the place of dreams and inspiration.*

*As you gaze out across the desert expanse, the eagle flies away, leaving you to dream. Tell yourself, "I am inspired to _____" and fill in the blank. (Speaking softly) "My dream is . . ." "I am inspired to . . ." (Pause.) As you imagine your dream becoming real, watch your inspiration take form. How does it unfold? What pictures do you see? When you have it clearly, signal me. (Pause, awaiting signals from the students.)*

*Repeat to yourself, "I have a dream. I am inspired." Now answer one more question for yourself: "How can this dream inspire me in my real world?" (Pause and close.)*

To bring students back to the classroom, ask them to open their eyes and stretch their arms and legs. Ask them to look all around the room. Have them share their experiences with partners.

Discuss these questions with students: Why is it important for people to have dreams or inspirations? What dreams do you have? What things in life inspire you? What answers did you receive from "How can this dream inspire me in my real world?" "How can we make dreams real?"

# Flying Further

- ★ Ask students to brainstorm and mind map all of the inspiring possibilities for their future. Have them share these dreams with a friend.

- ★ Have students envision a dream for the perfect world. What would it be like? How would we treat one another? Ask students to write a description or draw a picture. What is their role in this perfect world? What will they need to do in order to fulfill their part in a perfect world?

- ★ Explore the life of Martin Luther King, Jr. What was his dream? See if students can find threads of inspiration in Dr. King's life that encouraged him to continue dreaming his dreams. Have students explore the lives of other creative people and find out who or what inspired them: explorer Mary Kingsley or Roald

Amundsen, artist Pablo Picasso or Georgia O'Keeffe, musician J. S. Bach or Ludwig van Beethoven, leader Catherine the Great or Indira Gandhi, astronaut Edgar Mitchell or Sally Ride.

★ Have students research the ways that different cultures view sleeping dreams, where the people find inspiration, and how they set goals. Ask students to share their findings with the class.

★ Ask students to write down their sleeping dreams for a week. What are their dreams about? Do they have anything to do with goals or inspiration?

The following are related activities, developed by Caron Goode and Joy Watson (1992), that you can use in art and music.

★ Ask students to express the colors of their dreams using crayons, pastels, chalks, markers, or watercolors. They will use no words in the process, but will just allow the colors and the variations to express the inspiration.

★ Have students make collages that contain images of their inspirations or their dreams.

★ Discuss with students what songs they find inspiring. Over the next few days, have them listen to music and each find a song that is inspiring. Ask them to determine if it is the music, the words, or the mood that is inspiring. Can students name songs that inspire? Play some in class and discuss inspiration.

# 76 Moving into the Future

Sometimes the most difficult part of accomplishing a goal is envisioning the process of attaining it. In this activity students mime a special goal. The experience of acting out a goal can be a positive reinforcement that makes it easier for students to reach their goals. Students love the activity of miming and guessing what each other's mimes are.

## Activity

Ask students to sit quietly for a moment or two and think of a special activity or goal they would like to accomplish this year. Have them decide how they would mime their goal or activity. Give each student two or three minutes to present the mime to the rest of the class. Have the other students guess what is being mimed. For large classes, you may want to have the students do the activity in groups of six or seven.

> Perhaps the most important single cause of a person's success or failure educationally has to do with the question of what he believes about himself.
>
> —Arthur W. Combs

# 77 Totem Symbols

David Brewer

Establishing personal values and standards of behavior is an important part of developing character and a sense of pride in one's self. Children need to observe people whose behavior models admirable personality qualities. Parents and teachers provide living role models; folk stories, fairy tales, and some of today's television shows and movies give memorable examples.

Some American Indian traditions value animals as having great lessons to teach humans about relationships among living beings and about living in harmony with the Earth. For some native cultures, certain animals have come to symbolize specific qualities that people are to seek out, acquire, and perpetuate through the next generation by telling stories and serving as examples. Among the Ojibway people, for example, animals are used as totems, symbols for a family or clan.

The word *totem* is thought to have come from the same root as *dodum,* meaning "to fulfill," and *dodosh,* meaning "breast" or "that from which food comes." Totem therefore may mean "that from which I draw my purpose, meaning, and being."

In this activity, students study the nature and behavior of totem animals to see how those animals manifest the qualities the Ojibway have given them. You can use this activity as an opportunity for students to reflect on desirable character traits.

# Activity

Give students the following list of Ojibway totem animals and their character traits. (The list is also included in the appendix.) Have each student select an animal to be a totem animal or assign each student a totem animal you feel reflects his or her personality. If you are teaching young students, you may want to select six totem animals to study as a class.

Following are some ideas for projects students can do to study personality characteristics through totem animals.

- ★ Ask students each to research and write a brief report about one of the totem animal's habits and explain how these habits reflect the qualities observed and honored by the Ojibway tribe. Then have them each write a brief description of the totem animal's special quality and explain how this characteristic helps the animal to survive and live within its ecosystem.

- ★ Have students collect pictures and photos of their totem animals doing different activities; have them draw their animals. You might ask students to display the visuals on a bulletin board or mural, put them in a notebook, or make a collage to represent the animal.

- ★ Have students find American Indian stories or stories from another culture about the totem animal and share them with the class. Look for examples of the animal's Ojibway trait in each story and discuss the stories.

- ★ Ask each student to select an animal that is not on the list of Ojibway totems. Each student will explore the animal's habits and will find a character trait she or he feels the animal manifests in its behavior. The students will share their discoveries with the class and explain why they think the animal represents the quality they have given it.

- ★ Students can make a totem pole that includes four different totem animals whose qualities the students would like to develop. Have each student write a list of three things he or she can do to include each quality in his or her life.

# Ojibway Totem Animals and Qualities

| Animal | Quality | Animal | Quality |
|--------|---------|--------|---------|
| crane | leadership | hawk | foresight |
| eagle | courage, insight | seagull | grace, peace |
| loon | fidelity | black duck | depth |
| goose | prudence | sparrow hawk | perseverance |
| bear | strength, courage | moose | endurance, strength |
| marten | single-mindedness, judgment | wolf | perseverance, guardianship |
| lynx | determination | muskrat | endurance |
| beaver | resourcefulness, minding own business, | whitefish | abundance, fertility, beauty |
| sturgeon | depth, strength | pike | swiftness, elegance |
| merman | temptation | sucker | calmness, grace |
| mermaid | temptation | frog | transformation |
| water snake | willingness | catfish | breadth, scope |
| turtle | communication, messenger | rattlesnake | patience, slow to anger |

# 78 Direction Pointers

Emily Cummings

We have many choices in life. Like the point made by Scarecrow in the *Wizard of Oz*, some people like to go one way, and others like to go another. Learning to make our own choices not only requires a strong self-esteem but will also build our self-esteem as we make successful choices. This activity helps students look at choices.

## Activity

Ask students to think of an issue that they need to make a decision about. If students can't think of one, select a classroom problem and ask students to use it for their Direction Pointers activity. Have students spread the fingers of one hand wide and trace around the hand on a piece of paper. Ask students to brainstorm about their issues or problems and come up with five solutions. Some of these suggestions may seem silly, but they are all okay. Have the students write one choice by each finger on their drawings. Students now have five different solutions to their problems.

★ Ask students to play "What if . . . " with each of the choices and think about the possible outcomes of each choice. The students can write the possible outcomes of each choice on their Direction Pointers picture.

★ Ask students each to study their Direction Pointers and make a decision. Have them explain why they have made the choice they did.

Students can use this technique in the following situations:

## Deciding what they would like to be when they grow up

## Settling classroom disputes

## Resolving a dispute with a friend

## Reviewing other options in a situation in which they made a poor choice

# Flying Further

The following are related activities that you can use in history, ecology, and literature.

★ Use this activity to make classroom decisions about rules, projects, and special events.

★ Review a historical event and ask students to make a Direction Pointer about the different choices that the participants could have made. Was the choice the participants made the best? Why or why not?

★ Spend class time studying an ecological issue. Have students do the Direction Pointers activity about the choices we have. What do students think should be done about the problem?

★ Have students make Direction Pointers about a problem a character in one of your literature readings is having. The students read on and see what the character does in the story. Ask students if they think the character made the best choice. Did the students find a better choice?

# 79 Earth Visions

**Earth**

May Brewer

Our children will inherit planet Earth, including its gifts and its problems. We currently have a planet with significant survival issues. It is not only crucial that we begin to make changes to improve the health of our planet but we must actively teach our students that their actions will make a difference. Children seem to be aware of the current precarious position of the global environment. Actually, most children seem more willing than adults to make changes in their habits. After all, children have a vested interest in a healthy planet. Following are a number of ideas to reinforce the conviction that students' actions are important and will make a difference.

## Activities

The following activities were designed by Caron Goode and Joy Watson (1992).

- ★ As a class, study your local community to determine the condition of the environment and the amount of pollution. Have students make a list of suggestions for improvement, select one as a class project, and carry it out.
- ★ Have students make a list of what they can do at home to help the environment.
- ★ Have an environmental official talk to the class about what is being done to address local environmental concerns.
- ★ Have each student create an environmental notebook. Students can cut out current events stories from magazines and newspapers, write a personal plan for action, and write about their personal feelings on environmental issues.

# 80 Future Visions

Our world is quickly changing—the world we know today will be different tomorrow. People who are interested in understanding the range of possibilities for the future study trends in history, economics, and social structure. These futurists make predictions of what our world will be like. Looking toward the future allows us to see problems that we may be able to prevent. We can also prepare our homes, families, and communities to use our resources and energy in the most efficient ways.

We can look toward our personal future as well, predicting trends and making plans based on our past experiences. This activity explores the future.

## Activity

Give students resources about futuristics and allow them time to research and explore the topic. Ask students to make a list or mind map of aspects in today's world that they think will be different in twenty years. Ask them to consider such things as how people will travel in the future, what kind of clothes people will wear, what kind of work people will do, what environmental problems humans will be working with, and so on.

Students may draw pictures or a mural or build a clay sculpture of a future world scenario. Ask students to consider possibilities for their personal future. What kinds of jobs that they would like to do will be available in the future? Where do they think they might live? What activities would they like to do? Ask students to make a mind map or write a short future scenario for themselves.

## Flying Further

The following are related activities that you can use in science, language arts, history, and art.

★ Suggest to students that they find someone over 65 years old and ask that person to share the changes that have occurred during his or her life. The students should ask what the older person's perspective of the future is. Have students share with the class, write   a short report, or make a cassette recording of some part of the interview.

★ Ask students to read science fiction books about the future and select a scenario they think is possible. Read them part of *Twenty Thousand Leagues under the Sea* and make a list of things in the book that did become reality.

★ Have students design a future vehicle, kitchen, entertainment center, or classroom. They can make a drawing or write a report and share it with the class.

★ Ask students to research what the world was like one hundred years ago. Ask them to make a list of things that have changed since then. You may want them to pick just one topic to research.

> A great deal of research in cognitive psychology shows that the more actively you process information, the more you retain it.
>
> —David N. Perkins

# CHAPTER FOUR

# The Classroom Climate

*Giving people, young people, a loving philosophic base for understanding themselves in order to prepare them to be on solid emotional ground as adults is the most important thing we can do.*

—Edgar Mitchell

*The purpose of education is to nurture thoughtfulness. The lesser function of thinking is to solve problems and puzzles. The essential purpose is to decide for oneself what is of genuine value in life. And then to find the courage to take your own thoughts seriously.*

—Albert Einstein

*In the end we will conserve only what we love; we will love only what we understand; and we will understand only what we are taught.*

—Baba Dioum

As teachers, our job is not only to create a classroom environment that includes materials and resources for learning, but also to establish a learning climate where children feel they have positive support and direction, where each child can follow his or her unique learning journey with a sense of confidence and assurance. A supportive classroom climate provides students with a comfortable, safe environment that challenges them to learn but does not make them feel threatened. Stress can put our minds and bodies into a survival mode and actually turn off our creative and critical thinking abilities. This chapter includes activities to help you develop the supportive environment students need to feel they have freedom to fly.

# The Teaching Rhythm

A harmonious classroom climate begins with the teacher. A teacher's confidence, moods, and attitudes are reflected in his or her movements, speech, thoughts, and patterns of interaction. When a teacher's attitude is positive, encouraging, and accepting, students will feel good about themselves. When a teacher's attitude conveys excitement and dedication to teaching, students will feel good about the classroom and learning. In a positive classroom climate students will be able to respond to the teacher and the subject matter with focus and a desire to learn.

Teachers are frequently some of the most powerful role models students will have. Students are constantly observing a teacher's behavior and may "map" these patterns onto themselves. Years after students leave a classroom, they may still carry behavior patterns they observed in their teacher.

The success of our teaching and our value as role models depend to a great degree on our ability to be centered, to feel focused, and to be in harmony with our personal rhythms. The teacher's day can be stressful as he or she attempts to meet the needs of many students. The needs of caregivers in any field, at home or at work, must be met before they can be effective in their work. The following questions are designed to help you decide if your needs are being met and if you feel supported in your work.

- ★ Do you feel supported by the school administration?
- ★ Does your classroom have adequate space and materials to meet your teaching needs?
- ★ Does your teaching schedule provide you with the opportunities you need to reenergize yourself so you can meet the needs of students?
- ★ Does your classroom reflect the mood you want to set for your students?
- ★ Do you feel there is enough freedom in your curriculum to express your own creative ideas and teaching style?
- ★ Do you have time to meet the curriculum demands and requirements set by the administration?
- ★ Are there aspects of teaching you feel you need to know more about in order to do your job the way you would like to do it?
- ★ Do you enjoy being with students?
- ★ Do you find that parts of your school day are consistently difficult or trying?
- ★ Can you balance comfortably your home life, personal needs, and teaching demands?
- ★ Do issues from home end up being brought to the classroom?
- ★ Do classroom issues find their way into your home?

Your answers to these questions will help you isolate problems that may be disrupting your teaching rhythm and may be keeping the classroom climate from being the best it could be. You can resolve some classroom problems yourself; you may need to seek help from other people to find creative solutions to other problems. The problems that remain may require that you change your attitude. The Prayer of St. Francis points out simply and clearly that change is possible in all things, but it takes wisdom to recognize which changes should occur through efforts to change something else and which should involve internal changes.

The following activities were designed to help you maximize your teaching potential by focusing on your teaching goals, coordinating personal needs with schedule demands, and learning how to adjust your personal tempo.

# 81 The Teaching Connection

Sometimes the frustrations we experience in teaching can cause us to become disillusioned. We may not fully acknowledge our teaching accomplishments, or we become so lost in the hectic day-to-day schedule that we lose sight of the special meaning our teaching career holds for us. Unless we take the time to evaluate how much we have grown in our teaching, we may not realize how much we have accomplished or how successful we have been in reaching our goals. We may not even be sure of where we are going. This activity will help you focus on how you feel about your work, allow you to reflect on your teaching goals, and provide insights into your future directions.

## Activity

Draw three circles, approximately three to five inches in diameter, on a piece of plain paper. To fill in the first circle, think back to when you first started teaching and reflect upon your feelings using the following.

1. How did you feel?
2. What were your goals and aspirations?
3. Using colored markers, draw your feelings about your early teaching goals in the first circle. Use only colors, lines, and shapes (no symbols) in your drawing.

Circle #1

In the second circle, draw your feelings about your present teaching experience, keeping the following in mind:

1. How do you feel now about teaching?
2. What colors best depict your current emotions toward your profession?
3. Are the lines that reflect your feelings about teaching soft or jagged or both?
4. Draw your feelings about your present teaching experience. Again, use only colors, lines, and shapes.

To fill in the third circle, close your eyes and envision the future.

1. How would you most like to feel about teaching?
2. Imagine how you would feel if your teaching experience was the best it could be. Fill in the circle with the lines, shapes, and colors of future teaching goals.

When you are finished drawing spend a few moments reviewing your circles. What progression do you see through your teaching career? Which past goals and aspirations have you accomplished and which have you left behind? What do your feelings about your present teaching experience say to you? How can you make your present circle and experience match your future vision?

When you have reflected upon your teaching connection, you may want to make a list of what you have accomplished so far and a list of your goals for the future. Keep these lists handy so that you can add to them or read them periodically to refresh your memory.

When cut out and hung from a piece of wood or a coat hanger, your teaching connection circles can make a beautiful mobile that is also a lovely reminder of your teaching connection.

> Students are thinking all the time, but experience teaches us that, without reflection on what we do, we are not likely to benefit from our good thinking.
>
> —John Barell

# 82 | Where Does My Energy Go?

## Activity

Chapter 1 provides activities for students to reach inward and gain a stronger understanding of who they are and how they function. The Energy Cycles and Circles section is designed to help students discover their energy and attention patterns. If you did not do the activities to explore your energy and attention patterns when the students were exploring theirs, now is a good time to do the exercises yourself. They will give you a good picture of your personal energy flow and your rhythms of attention.

When you have completed the activities, take the time to define your energy and attention patterns clearly. Note the approximate times your highs and lows occur. Evaluate your class activities and determine which ones will require a great deal of your energy and which ones will use only a little of your energy. Look at your daily schedule and see where your energy goes.

★ Which activities are you doing during your high-energy period?
★ Which ones are scheduled during your low-energy times?
★ Are you teaching energy-demanding topics during your energy peaks?
★ Have you intuitively scheduled activities requiring little energy during your energy lulls?
★ Do you notice a difference in students' responses between the activities scheduled during your high-energy peaks and those scheduled during low-energy periods?

If you can adjust your schedule, experiment with changes in your activities to make your energy flow consistent with the energy needs of the schedule. I hope you can find a way to harmonize your energy rhythms with your workday schedule. But there may be some parts of your schedule you cannot change. If so, the Changing Tempos activity will provide you with ideas for perking up your energy.

# 83 Changing Tempos

After you have determined your personal rhythms of attention and energy you will have a clearer sense of your personal pace and the energy levels your work and home life require. Your personal rhythms may or may not match the flow of your workday and home life. Remember that you set the tone for the classroom and if you are feeling stretched and strained, chances are that your students will feel that way, also. Here are some ideas for changing your personal tempo to help you match your rhythms to the demands of your day.

## Activity

Look at the results of the previous activity to decide when your personal energy levels do not match the levels needed in your work or home life. Notice which parts of your day or class periods seem to have an energy slump. Notice which parts of the day are most challenging for you.

★ When do you need an energy lift?

★ When are your rhythms energetic?

★ When would a more relaxed state be beneficial to you and those around you?

Review your activities during the times of day when you feel you need a change of energy. Does your tempo need to increase or decrease during these times? The following ideas will help you adjust your energy levels to meet the needs of your schedule. For an energy lift, do one or more of the following:

★ In the background, play quiet music from the Sound Breaks lists or a favorite tape from your personal library that provides you with energy and excitement. Be careful about using energizing music in the classroom if you do not want to change the tempo of those around you in the same manner.

★ Take a body break and have the class do an energizing activity with you. I suggest one of the activities in Bumping the Blues, Sound Expressions, or Energy Infusions.

★ Make a conscious effort to add more inflection to your voice. Even if you don't lift your energy, you will increase students' attention levels and keep them from feeling your low energy.

★ Move to a different location in the room. Sometimes just a new view of things can perk your attention as well as redirecting your students' focus.

For an energy soother, do one or more of the following:

★ Quietly play music from the Sound Soothers lists when you want to relax. You may also check your personal library for musical selections that provide you with a sense of calm and relaxation.

★ Make a conscious effort to slow your breathing down, which will slow your brain waves and relax your body.

★ Take a moment when students are occupied and do an Imagining—close your eyes (if you dare) and imagine one of your favorite things. Spend a couple of minutes in this scene if possible.

★ Ask the class to do one of the Energy De-fusers with you.

Keep a daily journal of your discoveries about your energy patterns or make comments about your energy flow on your daily lesson plans. After you have experimented changing your tempo in the classroom, review your notes. Ask yourself the following questions:

★ How do you feel now during these points of changing energy?

★ What has assisted you most in altering your personal tempo?

# The Sound Environment

May Brewer

Recent research has greatly increased our knowledge and understanding of body-mind connections. We are now much more aware of the physical conditions that define an optimal learning situation. The use of music in the classroom has been determined to be highly effective for enhancing mental focus and concentration. Music can direct our energy levels so that our minds and bodies are in an optimal learning state. Music will enhance movement and imagery learning techniques. Finally, music has the ability to inspire us and create an atmosphere of warmth, comfort, safety, and enjoyment in the classroom.

Music is a dynamic, easy-to-use tool. I use music regularly in classes and workshops, and students' comments about its effectiveness are overwhelmingly positive. The following section provides activities that will prepare both students and teachers to use music in the classroom to help create an optimal learning experience. I include lists of suggestions (copies of the lists are also in the appendix), but you may very well have music in your personal collection that will work well in the classroom. Give your students and yourself a lift by experimenting with music in the classroom and take note of the changes you enjoy.

**Music in the classroom will do all of the following:**

★ *create a relaxed atmosphere*
★ *increase attention by creating a short burst of energizing excitement*
★ *release tension, especially if you move to it*
★ *enhance imagery activities*
★ *align groups*
★ *develop rapport*
★ *provide inspiration*
★ *add an element of fun*
★ *establish a positive learning state*
★ *provide a multisensory learning experience that improves memory*
★ *create a background sound that focuses concentration*
★ *accentuate theme-oriented units*

# 84 Focusing Sound: Making the Concentration Connection

Concentration requires focus. Accelerated learning techniques integrate the use of music into their methods because certain styles of music will harmonize brain and body rhythms and create an optimal learning state. Students can actually learn more quickly and with greater ease.

The balance of mind and body facilitated by concentration music relaxes students and provides a sense of calm that engenders confidence and comfort in learning tasks. Here are specific suggestions for using music for concentration and focus.

## Activities

Play one of the sound suggestions quietly as background music in the classroom when you need your students to focus. **Play the music**

- ★ *during a lecture*
- ★ *during independent work on projects*
- ★ *during quiet study time*
- ★ *during silent reading time*
- ★ *during focused cooperative learning projects*
- ★ *during work on creative projects*
- ★ *during a test*

## Sound Suggestions for Developing Focus

Music that develops focus is even and regular with no unexpected changes that could be distracting. The tempo is generally moderate to slow. A continuous flow of pace and melody will allow continuous flow of thought. Classical music from the baroque era has a reliable pulse, rhythm, and harmonic progression that enhances focus. Collections of baroque music recordings have been designed specifically to maintain continuity and provide a uniform tempo. Baroque recordings of entire concertos that use both fast and slow movements, however, have also been found to be effective for enhancing focus. Certain Mozart selections from the classical era will work well for concentration, too.

Vocal music with recognizable words should not be used. Gregorian chant, with Latin words and long breathing patterns, can relax the body while allowing the mind to be alert. Piano music has a special ability to bring focus inward.

## Piano

Lanz, David Nightfall. *Return to the Heart*
Winston, George. *December, Autumn*

## Flute

Nakai, Carlos. *Cycles, Earth Spirit*
Rainer, John. *Songs of the Indian Flute*

## Gregorian chant

Hildegard of Bingen. *A Feather on the Breath of God*
Rutter, John. *Brother Sun, Sister Moon*
Utrecht Students' Chamber. *Officinum Tenebrarum*

## Slow Baroque Music

Short Selections

Albinoni, Tomaso. Adagio in G Minor for Strings and Organ
Bach, Johann Sebastian. Air on a G String, "Jesu, Joy of Man's
    Desiring," "Sleepers Awake"
Pachelbel, Johann. Canon in D

Collections

Celestial Harmonies. Adagio I or II
LIND Institute. *Relax with the Classics,* Nos. 1–4 (Andante,
    Adagio, Pastorale, Largo)

## Baroque Selections with a Variety of Tempos

Bach, J. S. *Brandenburg Concertos,* especially no. 2
Barzak Educational Institute. *Baroque Music No. 1* or *Baroque
    Music   No. 2*
Campbell, Don. *Cosmic Classics* (side 1)
Concertos or sonatas by Johann Sebastian Bach, Arcangelo Corelli,
    George Frederick Handel, Pietro Locatelli, Georg Phillip
    Telemann, or Antonio Vivaldi
Handel, George Frederick. *Water Music, Royal Fireworks Suite*
Rutter, John. *The Handel Collection*
Vivaldi, Antonio. *The Four Seasons*

## Most recordings of the following Mozart selections

C Major Piano Concerto
Any of the Mozart divertimentos
*Eine Kleine Nachtmusik*
Prague and Haffner Symphonies
Rutter, John (conductor). *The Mozart Collection*

 # Sound Soothers: Music for Relaxation

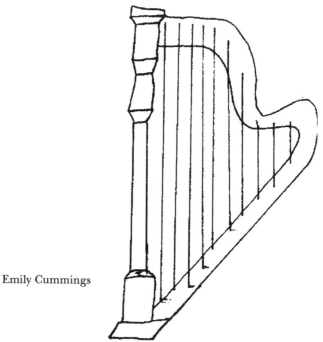

Emily Cummings

We can do many activities better when we are relaxed and calm. To keep an energy balance during the day we need our high energy periods interspersed with opportunities to relax and refocus. Students and teachers appreciate these sound soothers.

## Activities

Use soothing sound when you feel students need an opportunity to relax. Experiment with the following times:

★ **during independent work on projects**

★ **during quiet study time**

★ **during silent reading**

★ **during focused, cooperative-learning projects**

- during artwork or other creative projects
- during sessions when students are developing personal imagery
- during a special activity to relax students and relieve tension

# Sound Suggestions for Relaxation

The music that helps people concentrate will often work well as relaxation music. Certain music will move the listener even more deeply into a relaxation state, however. This music is often slower than the concentration selections. Consistency is important. A repeated slow pulsation will entrain the listener to a relaxed pace. A different but also effective style for relaxation creates a free-flow feeling without any discernible pulse. Harp, flute, electronic sounds, and string ensembles are very effective instruments for relaxation music.

Aeoliah. *Angel Love*

Campbell, Don. *Angels* (side 2), *Crystal Meditations, Runes* (for deep relaxation)

Chacra Artists. *New Age of Classics: Bach* (with ocean sounds)

Halpern, Steven. *Spectrum Suite, Dawn*

Horn, Paul. *The Peace Album*

Kobialka, Daniel. *Velvet Dreams* (string music)

Robertson, Kim. *Wind Shadows,* vols. 1 and 2 (Celtic harp)

Sill, Gary. *Pachelbel with Ocean*

# 86 | Sound Breaks: Music for Movement and Energy

Energizing music can help stimulate students and teachers during low-energy periods. We often learn and work better when we take a moment or two to release tension and energize ourselves. The use of one or two short selections works best to give people a quick charge that refreshes but does not overstimulate. Energizing music should be used sparingly to keep it effective.

## Activities

Play a short movement selection

★ at the beginning of the day to chase off the sandman

★ for a quick break after an hour or more of focused seat work

★ between subjects to make an energizing transition

★ whenever energy levels seem to be lagging

★ during the midafternoon, low-energy period

★ when bodies are feeling tense or tight

★ to celebrate the completion of a project

★ to build excitement for a specific activity

★ before a test to perk up attention

★ as a closure activity at the end of a day

# Sound Suggestions for Movement and Energy

For movement activities, music with a steady rhythm will help students feel comfortable in moving, will set a rhythm, and will keep energy levels high. Music with a high energy flow is just as effective as music with a constant heavy beat. Music with words will be just as effective as instrumental music. Sometimes the addition of lyrics is beneficial if the words are appropriate for the classroom.

Listen to a music selection before using it in class to make sure it will be appropriate for your activity.

Brubeck, Dave. "Take Five"
Joplin, Scott. Ragtime music

Lewis, Brent. *Earth Tribe Rhythms*

Louis Clark, Royal Philharmonic Orchestra. *Hooked on Classics*

Lynch, Ray. *Deep Breakfast*

Mannheim Steamroller. *Saving the Wildlife,* "Wolfgang Amadeus Penguin"

Rowland, Mike. *Fairy Ring*

Sousa, John Phillip. Marches

Strauss, Johann. Waltzes

Synchestra. *Mother Earth's Lullaby*

Tchaikovsky, Peter Illyich. Waltzes

Winter, Paul. *Earthbeat*

Yanni. *Keys to Imagination*

Experiment with lively Motown songs, 1950s rock n' roll, Celtic Irish music, disco or break-dance music, jazz, or exciting movie soundtracks.

> The most urgent need today is to restore the magic powers of love, confidence and belief in the perfectibility of humankind.
>
> —Robert Muller

# 87 Sound Images: Music for Imagery

Jenny Bissell

Sound holds great potential for creating mental images. How often has a piece of music brought back a memory or feeling for you? Play a music selection and see what pictures appear in your imagination. The use of images, or visual thinking, as Win Wenger calls it, is a powerful learning tool. Besides being enjoyable, the use of imagery in learning has been shown to improve memory and comprehension. When music is used with imagery, the experience becomes even more dynamic and powerful.

## Activities

The following list suggests opportune times to use imagery music in the classroom:

★ **while you lead students on a guided imagery journey about a curriculum topic**

★ **during an imagery review at the end of a class period**

★ **as you lead students through a guided visualization that reinforces students' abilities**

* during self-esteem–building activities when music will help inspire students

* while students are developing a creative writing theme or creative art project

# Sound Suggestions for Imagery

Music for imagery has diverse characteristics depending on its use. To provide background sound during a guided imagery, find music that is simple, flowing, and harmonious. You will need to choose long selections to avoid distracting breaks between cuts. If music is used as a stimulus for imagery but not as background sound for a guided visualization, music that is expressive, interesting, and variable will stimulate a greater variety of imagery.

## Guided Visualization Background Music

Bearns and Dexter. *Golden Voyage,* vols. 1–4

Halpern, Steven. *Soundwave 2000 Series: Creativity, Spectrum Suite*

Kobialka, Daniel. *Velvet Dreams*

Rowland, Mike. *Fairy Ring*

Sill, Gary. *Pachelbel with Ocean*

## Music to Stimulate Imagery

Debussy, Claude. *La Mer*

Gardner, Kay. *Rainbow Path*

Holst, Gustav. *The Planets*

Kitaro. *Silk Road Suite*

Mannheim Steamroller. *Saving the Wildlife*

Shardad. *Beauty of Love*

Sill, Gary. *Pachelbel with Ocean*

Winter, Paul. *Earthbeat, Wolf Eyes*

# 88 | Sound Connections

Throughout time, people have written songs that tell the story of their hearts. The connections these songs make for us can be powerful, moving, and inspirational. The poetry within the music can carry us through difficult times, lift us toward greater accomplishments, and allow us to open our hearts to one another.

## Activities

When classroom activities have become cognitively intense, take three minutes and play a song that will bring the class into a sound connection of feeling and caring. Play a sound connection song

★ to set a positive mood as students enter the classroom

★ to reinforce a learning theme

★ to give students a positive attitude just before a test

★ to lift and inspire students toward greater accomplishment

★ to reconnect students with goals and dreams

★ to emphasize self-worth

★ to bond students and help them feel a sense of classroom community

★ to celebrate accomplishment

★ as an inspiring closure at the end of the day

## Sound Suggestions for Inspiration

Sound connections are made through inspirational lyrics or sheer power of sound. The following songs can be used to make sound connections for self-worth, cooperation, inspiration, and caring. Don't forget to ask students to bring in songs that they find inspirational and moving.

Armstrong, Louis. "What a Wonderful World"

Cara, Irene. "What a Feeling" (from *Flashdance*)

Collins, Judy. "Both Sides Now"

Denver, John. "I Want to Live"

Diamond, Neil. "He Ain't Heavy"

Flack, Roberta. "Reach Out and Touch Someone"

Franklin, Aretha. "Look to the Rainbow"

Houston, Whitney. "One Moment in Time," "Greatest Love of All"

Ingram, James, and Linda Ronstadt. "Somewhere Out There"

Jackson, Michael. "The Man in the Mirror," "It's as Easy as 1, 2, 3"

King, B. B. "Stand by Me"

King, Carole. "You've Got a Friend"

McFerrin, Bobby. "Don't Worry, Be Happy"

Any recording of "Man from La Mancha" (The Impossible Dream)

Midler, Bette. "From a Distance," "Wind beneath My Wings"

Pomeranz, David. "It's in Every One of Us"

Quist, Rob. "Back in Harmony"

Simon, Carly. "Let the River Run"

Simon, Paul, and Garfunkel, Art. "Bridge over Troubled Waters"

Sonny and Cher. "The Beat of a Different Drummer"

South, Joe. "Walk a Mile in My Shoes"

The following albums have a number of appropriate songs on them:

Denver, John. *Seasons of the Heart*

Grammer, Red. *Teaching Peace*

Jackson, Michael. *Heal the World*

Lasar, Mars. *Olympus* (instrumental)

Lynch, Ray. *Deep Breakfast* (instrumental)

*The 1988 Summer Olympics,* especially "One Moment in Time"

Tesh, John. *The Games* (instrumental music from sports games)

# Bonding: The Human Connection

The strength of the human connection has been revealed time after time in history. "Together we stand, divided we fall" speaks to us of the potential created when people work together for a common cause. The spirit somehow becomes stronger when one person recognizes that he or she is bonded with another person—woven into the fabric of life through a human connection.

A classroom that emanates a spirit of support—where all the participants feel bonded to one another in the sharing of a mutual experience—is a classroom with a resonance that truly re-sounds with the energy of life. The following activities offer opportunities to reaffirm the bonds of student with teacher, the bonds of student with student, and the self-worth of each individual.

# 89 Pass It On

This activity has been adapted from an activity created by Teresa Benzwie (1988). People of all ages appreciate this activity because it allows us to take a brief moment to share with each other, refocus, remember the importance of community, and relax! Use it to start or end a class session, or slip it in during an intense work session as a break.

## Activity

Ask your students to stand in a circle with you. Choose one of the positive reinforcements from the list below and do it to the student standing next to you.

- ★ a hand squeeze
- ★ a hug
- ★ a back rub
- ★ a smile
- ★ a pat on the back
- ★ a thumbs-up sign
- ★ a "give me five"
- ★ an imaginary gift (mime the outline of the gift and the act of handing it to the next person)
- ★ a round of applause
- ★ a thanks for a good day

Have that student pass the reinforcement to the next student. The students continue passing the positive reinforcement until it has gone completely around the circle and everyone has given and received a special reinforcement.

> We all make mistakes. But to commit a wrong, to lower the dignity of a child and not be aware that the dignity has been impaired, is much more serious than the child's skipping words during reading.
>
> —Clark E. Moustakas

# 90 Kindness Coupons

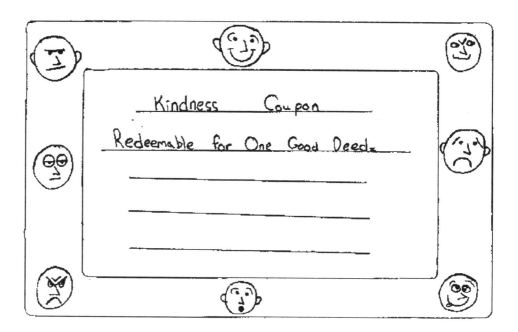

Emily Cummings

This activity is an enjoyable way to teach students that one good turn deserves another!

## Activity

Make a "kindness coupon" for each student. Tell students that when they need a favor, they can put their kindness coupons out on their desks to signal that they need a favor. Other students can respond to the request by asking how they can help. Whoever does the favor keeps the coupon. Since this person has done a good turn, he or she deserves one in return. The student who received the favor no longer has a kindness coupon and must do a good turn for someone else in order to get a coupon to use later.

# 91 The Something-to-Do Box

This activity adds a bit of spontaneity and the element of surprise to bonding activities. The Something-to-Do activities are wonderful time fillers for those moments when you have to wait five minutes for the bell to ring and you have an antsy class. These are also great ideas for substitute teachers who are often left with undefined time. The excitement of this activity comes when a student pulls a suggestion from the Something-to-Do box; no one knows what it will be but everyone knows it will be fun! Be sure to add new suggestions periodically so that there is always an air of suspense.

## Activity

Decorate a box that you can call the Something-to-Do box. Cut a hole in the top big enough for a hand to fit into. Write a few activities on pieces of paper and slip them in the box. After students have a feel for the kind of activities that are in the Something-to-Do box, you can ask them to add their own suggestions. Following are some activities to start with; you can write the titles on the slips of paper.

★ *Play Twenty Questions.*

Select a student to be the subject for Twenty Questions. Have the class ask you twenty questions about the person's personality, appearance, skills, and other attributes. Answer the questions and see if the class can guess which student you have in mind.

★ *Conduct.*

Play a selection of movement music or lively inspirational music and have everyone conduct to the music using hands, elbows, knees, hips, toes, ears, and other body parts!

★ *Tell a riddle or a joke.*

Keep a book of riddles and jokes handy and share them with the students.

★ *Sing a campfire song.*

Ask the students to pick a song and sing it. Clint Collins, a favorite sixth-grade teacher at Petersen Elementary School in Kalispell, Montana, has a collection of fun, sing-around-the-campfire songs about crazy kid things—the silly, gooey, gushy, scary kinds of songs. His students love to sing them!

★ *Use the box to introduce some of the short activities or part of a longer activity from this book.*

You might try Pass It On, Lions and Tigers and Bears, Oh My! I've Got to Hand It To You! Bumping the Blues, or Imaginings.

Tell students that the Something-to-Do box will hold suggestions for short activities that the class can do together when there are a few spare moments.

---

The whole art of teaching is only the art of awakening the natural curiosity of young minds.

—Anatole France

---

# 92 The Aha! Principle

Creative problem solving includes the following steps:

**Preparation:** gathering information and exploration

**Incubation:** a period of processing in the mind and body

**The Aha!:** an exciting point of insight

**Verification:** ensuring the integrity of an insight

**Implementation:** putting the information and insights into a usable framework

Without being conscious of it, we use the creative process in many ways throughout the day. We can recognize the Aha! stage as the time when a creative idea, the perfect solution to a problem, or an exciting insight comes to us. We are often not even thinking about the problem when our Aha! hits us.

When we have an Aha! in our learning process we are excited about what we learn. When we have an Aha! about ourselves, the revelation can be transformational. The following Aha! activities provide ways for students to understand the Aha! and to celebrate learning Ahas! in the classroom.

## Activity

Share the creative problem-solving process with students and read the Aha! rap that follows to the class. (The rap is also included in the appendix in case you wish to copy it.) Note that the Aha! Aha! Aha! Aha! section of the chorus can be a part the entire class does on your cue. Saying these Ahas! with energy and excitement will set the mood for the rest of the Aha! rap. Ask students to think about the last time they had an Aha! and to share the event with the class or partners. Ask students to think about when and where they most often get their Ahas! and make mind maps of these places. Common situations for Ahas! include while taking a shower or bath, while riding in a car or walking to school, while waking up or just before falling asleep, while cleaning your room or doing some kind of routine task, while exercising, while exploring nature. Share with students that Ahas! are an exciting part of the classroom and lifelong learning. They are gifts to be celebrated. Even more important, if we can make sure that we have the time and space in our lives to encourage them, our learning and living will be more interesting and exciting.

Use the following classroom activities to explore, encourage, and celebrate Ahas! in the classroom:

★ Have the students do an Aha! survey of their family and friends and see where people get most of their Ahas! Students might also ask the people they survey what the people's biggest Aha! has been.

★ Conduct an activity with the class to solve a community problem. Brainstorm solutions, mind map ideas, and ask students to incubate the problem and share their Ahas! with the class. Make a list of the Aha! solutions and present these ideas to the appropriate people in the community.

★ Jo Ellen Hartline (1990) has developed a way to honor Ahas! in the classroom. Hartline told her students that any time one of them got an Aha! during class work, she or he was to exclaim Aha! and the class would stop and celebrate the Aha! by clapping, cheering, and expressing appreciation of the Aha!

★ Practice brainstorming techniques—present a problem to the class and ask students to incubate the idea over part of the day. Tell them that it is okay to share *any* idea while brainstorming and that sometimes the craziest ideas have a little piece of the best answer in them. Suggest that the solutions in this session be as wild and crazy as possible. Later in the day come together in a circle and have students share their Ahas! by saying "Aha!" and telling their crazy idea. Write the solutions on a mind map and when all the crazy ideas are up, go back over them and see if there are some ideas within the crazy thoughts that might work with a little revision.

★ Ask students to research an inventor, leader, or other person in history who had an Aha! about something that changed the course of history. Share the reports in class.

## Aha!!

By Chris Brewer, with Jean Houston

*Chorus:*
The answer is there for all to see.
It lies inside of you and me
And when we hear what it has to say
We see the start of a brand new day!
Aha! Aha! Aha! Aha!

212

But let's get back to reality.
It's not my problem, don't you see?
And when it comes 'round to me
I don't have authority.
We're not ready for change.
We're too busy for that.
People will laugh.
It will probably fall flat!
We've always done it this way before,
But we can't seem to get our foot in the door.
Oh how hard do we fight
To keep old patterns in our sight!

*(Chorus)*

The new idea that you submit—
Just send it out in triplicate.
It's kicked upstairs to you know who.
The word comes down—Catch 22!!
Subsection 1, Paragraph 3,
Item 9, Addendum B.
See above and what do you know—
It says up there to see below!

*(Chorus)*

Creativity can open the door
And soon you'll find more and more.
So when you need to make a change
You'll find a way to rearrange.
You can whistle a tune
Or doodle till noon.
Oh you'll find a way
To make work play

*(Chorus)*

Make the time to incubate.
You'll find the answers are first rate.
You can make the problems blow away
If creativity has its say.
Believe in yourself and your insight.
There's lots of ways to make things right.
You're as creative as you feel.
It's as easy as that . . . what a deal!

*(Chorus)*

Aha! Aha! Aha! Aha!


**Note:** Verses 4 and 5 are by Jean Houston, adapted from
"SYS-TEM" (Brewer and Campbell [1991]).

# 93 Talking Time

In one of my education courses there was a teacher who had taught junior high for thirty-five years. Wanting to draw on his expertise of how to work with this sometimes-troubled age group, I asked him what he felt was the most important thing he did to help him connect with his students. His reply was "cruising," which he defined as walking around the room and talking one-on-one with students while they were working independently or reading. While he might have used this time for grading papers or preparing a lesson plan, in the long run he may have gained much more through this simple bonding technique.

Talking with students about schoolwork and related activities is important, but you can also use the time to talk about other areas students are interested in. Even if the topic seems far removed from schoolwork, this kind of interest and communication may be the factor that changes a student who feels alienated and struggles with your teaching into a student who is willing to work with you to improve his or her learning abilities.

Although you may feel that you don't have time to talk to each student in this way, the idea of taking five minutes for each student every week may amount to a total of only two hours per week. Here are some suggestions for finding ways and times to connect personally with students each week.

# Activities

- ★ Cruise. Simply walk around while students are working independently and visit with as many students as you can.
- ★ Set up an appointment calendar on your desk where students who feel they have a very specific need to speak with you can sign up for a time you set aside for this purpose. For example, you might set aside one lunch period a week, one day of recesses, or a half hour two days a week when students are normally working independently. Make this a special time for teacher-student talks.
- ★ Once a week, take a walk around the school when you are on your lunch break. Let students know that you would enjoy company if someone would like to walk with you. You may find that you come to cherish the exercise, to welcome the break from a hectic school schedule, and to appreciate the change from the regular discussions in the teacher's lounge. There is also something special about a leisurely walk with another person that encourages discussions too valuable to miss.
- ★ If one or two students avoid contact with you, a little extra effort can make them feel special. Write the student a note that says, "I'll meet you by the flagpole at 12:15—let's take a walk." Soon you may find you are getting similar notes back.

# 94 Lions and Tigers and Bears, Oh My!

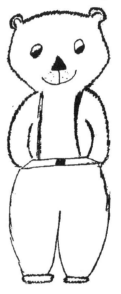

Stacey Brown

We are never too old to appreciate the value of a hug! In fact, hugs may get better as we age. Children are much more likely to grab a passing hug than an adult, so adults may get hugged only rarely.

One of the strongest human connections comes from the language of touch. Dr. Sid Simon has researched touch extensively and considers it to be a basic human need. Teachers, of all people, recognize the value of touch. Who has not seen a student respond positively to a hand placed on the shoulder as reinforcement for a job well done? What elementary teacher has not been almost bowled over by a group of wiggly, huggly bodies excited to see you?

But touching has become a touchy topic in today's world. Dr. Simon feels that if we taught and practiced safe touch at home and elsewhere, there would be less unsafe touch in the world. Touch can have a negative connotation for some students, however. I still remember one rather troubled boy who told me not to touch him when I lightly laid my hand on his shoulder as a gentle reminder of his manners. Touch has become such a controversial issue that some schools have adopted a no-touch policy.

You must judge for yourself how much touch to include as a way to bond in your classroom. Here are some ideas for safe touch in the classroom and some suggestions for replacing touch in those times and places where touch is not allowed.

# Activities

★ *I coined the acronym HUGGS to explain the value of hugs: Having U Give and Get Support.*

You can tell students the acronym and then develop a HUGGS network. Learn and share different kinds of hugs: big squeezy bear hugs, quick snatch hugs, rocking hugs, pat-the-back hugs. See what kinds of hugs students can make up. Have periodic HUGGS networking and suggest that everyone give someone else a particular style of hug. You can also have students tell partners the kind of hug they feel they need at the time. Students respond well to this activity and soon feel comfortable asking for some HUGGS networking when they need it.

★ *Place warm, fuzzy stuffed animals in accessible places in your room.*

There are wonderful, lifelike replicas available. Let students know that stuffed animals need at least ten hugs a day to be happy, and encourage students to pick up, hold, and snuggle with a stuffed animal regularly. If you notice a child in need of hugs, let her or him know which animal is short of hugs for the day and ask the student if she or he can supply some of the stuffed creature's hugs.

Surprisingly enough, though teddy bears are a long-time favorite, I have found that stuffed ducks are a wonderful hugging animal because of their shape. They can be cradled in one arm while the other hand strokes the body. Also, older students feel that ducks are less childish.

Your lions and tigers and bears in the classroom also offer opportunities for creating classroom stories (some of these creatures manage to develop wonderful personalities). Stuffed creatures can also be used in ecology and science studies (no dissecting please!), for creative writing material, and as art models. Oh my!

★ *Play Lions and Tigers and Bears, Oh My! when hugs are needed.*

In a large space have students link arms in lines of four, act really scared, and chant "Lions, and tigers, and bears. Oh, my!" as they "follow the yellow brick road" across the room together.

★ *Do group hugs, or "huggles," as my friend Ed Clark calls them.*

All it takes is a mass of huggly bodies that are willing to stand in a circle, place their hands on one another's shoulders, and make the circle as small as it can be.

★ *Touch is a strong acknowledgment tool.*

When you want to affirm a student's actions, place a hand lightly on his or her shoulder and accompany the touch with words of praise. When you do not want to encourage a student's inappropriate behavior, such as when she or he is crying or being self-pitying, be very careful not to anchor the behavior with touch. Instructors at SuperCamp are told to be compassionate from a distance when students are in one of these states, and to wait until students have come up with a positive solution to a problem or at least have indicated that they feel able to find a solution. Only then will the instructor anchor the student's behavior with a light touch on the shoulder and an encouraging statement.

> There are people whose feelings and well-being are within my influence. I will never escape that fact.
>
> —Hugh Prather

# The Learning Space

Emily Cummings

Paul MacLean's research on the triune brain has taught us a great deal about the various levels of brain function. At the most basic level, our reptilian brain accounts for our immediate survival needs and is especially concerned with space and territory. Our limbic brain handles emotional aspects of living, and our neocortex is the brain structure at which high-level cognitive and creative thought manifests.

Behavioral studies have revealed that we will have difficulty reaching the cognitive levels of thought if we feel our survival is threatened or our emotional state is not in balance. Our physical surroundings greatly influence our ability to learn. An uncomfortable or unfamiliar environment may trigger our reptilian or limbic brain into a survival mode and inhibit higher levels of thinking.

The following activities allow students to explore their learning space, to help make the classroom comfortable, and to develop learning space to the fullest and most productive use.

# 95 Searching through Space

This activity is a good get-acquainted activity for the beginning of the year. If students have questions about the room before they do a space search, they will have very few by the time they are done.

## Activity

Explain to students that they will be exploring the classroom with a variety of their senses. Begin by asking students to close their eyes and become aware of the classroom's sound environment by sitting quietly for three minutes and listening carefully to all the sounds they can hear.

At the end of three minutes ask students to share the sounds they heard. When you have finished the sound explorations or on another day, do a texture search. Ask students to take ten minutes to make rubbings of the various textures they find around the room. They will make rubbings by laying a lightweight paper (photocopy paper will work) on a surface and lightly rubbing a pencil or crayon over the top of the paper. The texture of the surface will create an interesting design on the paper. Students can each share one of their favorite rubbings and see if the class can guess where the texture came from. You can also make a classroom texture quilt by having each student cut a square of her or his favorite design, then tacking the squares together on a bulletin board. Explore the room visually for shapes. Ask students to do one or more of the following:

- ★ make a list of all the circle-shaped objects they find in the room
- ★ make a shape map that shows the major shapes they would see if they were looking down from the ceiling
- ★ go on a fifteen-minute treasure hunt for the following: three red objects, two squares, the largest triangle in the room, one item with polka dots, something that looks like a pyramid or mountain, and a circle within a circle

You may want to ask students to find one object in the room to explore fully with all the senses. Students can report back to the class or share with a partner.

# Flying Further

The following are related activities that you can use in science and history.

- ★ Add extra fun to this activity by "planting" course-related items. For example, if you are studying an animal in science, you can plant several representations of the animal in the room and see how many students can find them.
- ★ Begin a history unit by planting clues about the era or event you will be studying. See how many clues the students can find. Share the clues and see if students can guess what the unit is. For example, to study the Declaration of Independence you might plant  a plumed pen, a blank paper rolled up and tied with a ribbon, a defunct firecracker, a biography of Thomas Jefferson, and a map  of the United States in 1776.

# 96 | Personal Space Stretch Dance

This activity was developed by Teresa Benzwie (1988). Personal space includes all the space a person can reach from one position. This activity allows students to stretch and move in their personal space and is a helpful beginning for many movement lessons.

## Activity

Play movement music. Ask students to sit in spaces by themselves far enough away from anyone else so that they cannot touch one another. Ask students to reach their hands and arms slowly out to explore the space around them. Tell students to explore all of the space to the front, back, sides, and above and below them.

Repeat the exploration using legs to stretch and explore. Have students stretch in all possible positions, one arm or leg at a time, alternating arms and legs, then both together. Move arms and legs overhead, to the sides; cross them. Find new ways to stretch.

Have students slowly move into a standing position. Ask students to remain in one place while they stretch their arms and bodies in all directions and explore all the space around them. Ask students to stretch, twist, and bend slowly in a stretch dance. Have them keep their feet as stationary as possible but allow the movements to become one continuous flow.

> A genuine definition of intelligence based on an understanding of the capacity of the human brain and mind must include a broader understanding of how our brain organizes the "stuff of life" and then must leave room for discovering what we are capable of becoming.
>
> —Renate Nummela Caine and Geoffrey Caine

# 97 Finding Your Space

The next two activities give students a chance to find a special place to reflect and escape. Everyone needs a private space at some time, and these activities will help students realize that they can "take a little space" when they feel they need to.

## Activity

Ask students to find individual places in the room where they feel the most comfortable. Let them know it can be a place to sit, lie, or stand. Play concentration or relaxation music while students search for their spaces. Let students know that they are not to talk during this activity. Suggest that when students have found their special places, they can simply enjoy them until every student has located a special place.

When everyone has a special place, ask students to share what they like about their spaces. Students can return to their special places to reflect or to spend quiet time. If you need to take a short, reflective break from class work and feel as though students could use some time alone, turn off the lights, request silence, and ask students to go to their special places for five minutes. Students often greatly appreciate quiet time alone during a busy day and return to their school work refreshed and ready to learn. At some point, you may want to give students the option of finding a new special place.

> The strength of a man's position in the world depends on the degree of adequacy of his perception of reality. The less adequate it is, the more disoriented and hence insecure he is and hence in need of idols to lean on and thus find security. The more adequate it is, the more can he stand on his own two feet and have his center within himself.
>
> —Erich Fromm

# **98** Hideout Happiness

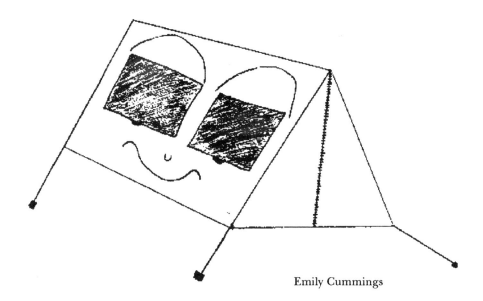

Emily Cummings

Every child loves a fort or a hideout! There is something special about spaces that children create for themselves. The human need for time alone is rarely fulfilled in the school classroom. Some children may not have spaces to themselves at home, either. In this activity, students will create their own hideout—a special place where they can go when they need a few minutes alone.

## Activity

Explain to students that they are going to make a hideout for the classroom. This place is a special place where students can go for five minutes if they need to be alone. Get a large appliance box and cut a doorway in it. Let students decide how they want to decorate it and develop an art project around making the hideout feel comfortable. Students can work in groups on different aspects: outside decorations, inside decorations, "comfort" items (pillows, blankets, rugs, and so on). When the box is complete the class can give the hideout a name and help you make rules for its use.

# 99 | The Kid-Designed Classroom

There are many things that you need in the classroom. As teachers, we often decide what to put in the room and how the room will be organized. Students also have ideas about how to use classroom items to make learning interesting and exciting. The students may also have a feeling for where items should be placed to be most accessible. By incorporating students' input into the classroom design, we allow them to take responsibility for structuring their learning process. In this activity, you and your students will co-create a learning space.

## Activity

Explain to students that the classroom is their learning space and that together you are going to make it the most comfortable, functional, and interesting room possible. Explain that you will probably experiment with different ways of arranging the classroom, but the whole class will help decide what arrangement offers the most effective environment to learn in.

As a class, make a list or mind map of items that students need for learning. You will ask students how they learn best.

★ Do some students appreciate a comfortable chair or couch to read in? If so, perhaps the room could include one.
★ Are animals and plants important? Will the classroom include a class pet or a terrarium?
★ What do students feel is the best seating arrangement to help them learn? A circle? Rows? A square or several squares?
★ Who needs space to keep from talking to others and how can they get it?
★ Do students like independent learning centers?

When students have answered these questions, list different ways to arrange the room. Select a method to begin with and draw a map on the board so students can help move chairs, desks, books, and other materials. If you teach older students, you might also consider having them form committees to decide how specific aspects of the room can be arranged (desk committee, books and learning materials committee, art center committee, learning center committee, and so on).

Make a response chart on the bulletin board where students can write what they like and don't like about the arrangement during the next two weeks. When two weeks are up, read the comments, decide what needs to change, and develop another plan. You may need to adjust a few times during the first two months, but students will eventually find a comfortable design. Encourage students to add new ideas throughout the year as they find new and interesting items to add to the classroom.

# Flying Further

The following are related activities that you can use in social studies, history, current events, and mathematics.

- ★ Ask students to research schools in other countries to see how classes are structured and what the classrooms look like. Students can make reports and draw pictures to share.
- ★ Have students find old pictures and photographs of schools from different historical eras and share how schools have changed in the last 100 years.
- ★ Find articles in education magazines that talk about various learning techniques, such as accelerated learning or cooperative learning, and share these with the class. Have students research the Montessori and Waldorf methods of education. How are classrooms structured in these methodologies? Are there some aspects of these techniques that could be easily incorporated into your classroom structure?
- ★ If you teach older students, have them use cardboard and construction paper or clay to make a scale model of a room from a design on paper.

> **When one has the need to learn and is free to choose what to learn, the knowledge acquired becomes meaningful and a source of satisfaction.**
>
> —Roy Jose De Carvalho

# 100 The Weather Report

Aimee Van Antwerp

There's no way around the fact that some days are better than others. Sometimes we just need a little space to feel angry or sad or frustrated. When we've had some time to revel in our moodiness, we can return to interacting happily with others. The following activity gives students permission to take space for themselves when they feel they need it. By the way, this also works for teachers.

## Activity

Explain to students that all people sometimes need a little time to themselves. Sometimes experiencing a feeling quietly by ourselves for a short time will allow us to move past it and go on to other things. At other times, we may just feel grouchy, and then it's only fair to warn others to give us a little room. Let students know that if they feel as though they need some personal space, they can give a weather report so that other students will know to leave them alone. Students can draw a weather scene that depicts their mood or write simply "storm warning" on a piece of paper and hang it on their desks. When they feel better, students can change their weather report to partly cloudy, scattered showers, or clear skies and sunshine! Besides helping to keep classroom harmony, this activity teaches students to be considerate of others.

# 101 Getting "A"-cclimated

Amanda Owens

To become acclimated means to get used to a particular climate, environment, or situation. This activity helps students to acclimate their classroom learning efforts so they match your learning expectations. When students can do this, they are more likely to be in your "A"-grade climate, or "A"-cclimated.

The optimal classroom climate encourages students to give their best efforts all of the time. Students know when they have given their best effort and when they haven't. I always like to ask my students to give themselves a grade for their efforts at the end of a semester. Although students occasionally give themselves A's when they don't deserve that grade, I have found that students will most often reflect their efforts accurately. I don't always give students the same grades they give themselves, but self-grading gives me the opportunity to let them know how to direct their efforts to meet my expectations. Also, I can always give them an "A" for effort!

In this activity, I take giving students the opportunity to appraise their efforts one step further. This method of evaluation lets both the student and teacher know how effort and expectation match on a regular basis. Another benefit to this activity is that it encourages cooperation between student and teacher to make the student's learning experience the best possible.

# Activity

Regularly ask students to give themselves an effort grade. Let them know that you get out of life what you put into it. Learning is the same way. The more effort they put in, the more understanding they get out. You can draw an analogy between life and a measuring cup. When you put two cups of water in the cup, you get two cups out. When you put one-quarter cup in, that's all you're going to get out of it! On class papers or projects where you would like to know how much effort students feel they are putting into their learning, ask them to draw pictures of cups that represent effort. The students will draw marks that represent how much liquid is in the cup, or how much effort they feel they put into the project. Let them know that their evaluation won't affect their grades, but it will let you know more about their potential. If they aren't able to put energy into the project for some reason, you will know it and realize that they can do better. You may even give them a second chance to "do their best" on a project when they are more able to put full energy into it. You can also show students how much better their work is when they pour on the effort than when they put only a drop of effort into their work.

# Postscript

## Taking Flight!

To spread our wings and to lift our bodies into the air require physical strength.

But to take flight—to believe that we have the ability to move with the wind, to stay in flight, and to return to land—requires a strength of the spirit.

We do not know whether our children will fly or fall. Yet to have faith in them—to give them wings and pass on to them the spirit of life—is to give our children the freedom to fly!

# APPENDIX

# Materials Used in Activities

# ............ Movement List............

**ANGRY:** How would you feel if you overheard someone saying something untrue about you?

**JOYFUL:** How did you feel when you learned to ride your bicycle or reached some other goal?

**SAD:** How did you feel when a good friend moved away or a pet died?

**EXCITED:** How did you feel when you found out your family was going to do something special?

**SNEAKY:** How did you feel when you tried to steal a cookie when no one was looking?

**LONELY:** How do you feel when you are left alone and you don't want to be?

**PEACEFUL:** How do you feel when you are snuggled in bed at the end of a great day?

**SICK:** How do you feel when you have the sniffles or the flu?

**HEALTHY:** How do you feel when you have been eating foods that are good for you and you've had plenty of sleep?

# Individual Identity Profile

For _____

          Name            Grade      Date       Submitted by

*Please rate your child's strengths in the following areas using the 0–5 scale provided, with 5 being the highest rating.*

|  | 0 | 1 | 2 | 3 | 4 | 5 |
|---|---|---|---|---|---|---|

### Linguistic Intelligence
Verbose—enjoys talking and playing with words
Enjoys writing; is fluent and expressive
Reads a lot for pleasure and information

### Musical Intelligence
Sings, hums, whistles a lot (on key)
Enjoys listening to a variety of music; notices various sounds
Plays instruments; makes sounds; feels rhythms

### Logical-Mathematical Intelligence
Curious; asks many questions
Collects, counts, compares, sorts, categorizes, and studies things
Plays with numbers; enjoys arithmetic "problems"

### Spatial Intelligence
Remembers landmarks, places visited
Knows directions; can draw and follow maps
Enjoys and is good at drawing, painting, sculpting
Is clean, neat, orderly

### Bodily-Kinesthetic Intelligence
Graceful, agile use of body
Expressive with dance, gymnastics, gestures, mime, athletics
Handles objects skillfully; can fix things

### Personal Intelligence
Understands and likes self; controls emotions
Self-confident; plans; organizes; uses initiative, persistence, work
Honesty and integrity; zest for life; thankful; appreciative

### Social Intelligence
Kind; friendly; loving; caring; generous; courteous
Leadership/Followership
Listens attentively; demonstrates empathy/respect
Is sensitive to others' feelings

### General Intelligence
Creative; inventive; imaginative
Sense of humor
Money management/thrift
Hobby or expertise in a particular field of knowledge

# Heritage Treasure Hunt List

1.  Where was your father born?

2.  Where was your mother born?

3.  On a map, locate where one of your grandmothers lived when she married your grandfather.

4.  Find out how the family of your grandfather celebrated the birth of your father. (What traditions were prominent in the culture of your grandfather for celebrating the birth of a child?)

5.  What was your mother's or father's favorite food as a child?

6.  On a map, trace the path of your father or grandfather through all the different places he lived.

7.  What language did one of your great-grandmothers speak?

8.  Ask your grandmother to sing one of her favorite childhood songs and write down the words. Or see if your mother remembers a song her mother sang to her.

9.  Find out which of your family's traditions was passed down to your family by a grandparent.

10. What is the history of your family name? What country is it from? Does it have a specific meaning in the language of this country? Has the name been changed?

# Natural Expressions

| Content Message | Emotion | Body Movements |
|---|---|---|
| I love to eat apples. | joy | lively |
| My foot hurts. | pain | restless |
| I am really upset about what happened. | anger | tense |
| I don't like to go into the hall when it is dark. | fear | cringing |
| I'm concerned about getting home late. | worry | jittery |
| I feel uncomfortable about eating the candy. | guilt | nervous |
| I wish my dog hadn't died. | sadness | limp |
| I can't believe I said what I did! | embarrassment | timid |
| I know I can pass the test! | confidence | strong |
| I'm so glad we can go to the circus! | happiness | energized |

# Mixed Messages

| Content Message | Emotion | Body Movements |
|---|---|---|
| I love to eat apples. | pain | restless |
| My foot hurts. | joy | jittery |
| I am really upset about what happened. | happiness | limp |
| I don't like to go into the hall when it is dark. | guilt | strong |
| I'm concerned about getting home late. | confidence | lively |
| I feel uncomfortable about eating the candy. | fear | energized |
| I wish my dog hadn't died. | embarrassment | tense |
| I can't believe I said what I did! | anger | cringing |
| I know I can pass the test! | sadness | nervous |
| I'm so glad we can go to the circus! | worry | timid |

The following is from Brewer and Campbell (1991, p. 182).

# My Discoveries

Name _____ Date _____

Today I made these discoveries:

Reading

Spelling

Language Arts

History, Social Studies

Science

Math

Music, Art

P.E., Health

# Home and Needs

The following list of Earth/home systems and human needs can be used to direct and categorize students' ideas during the mind mapping.

| **Earth/Home Systems** | **Human Needs** |
|---|---|
| Air: Atmosphere | Shelter |
| Land: Lithosphere | Food |
| Water: Hydrosphere | Transportation |
| Energy: Heliosphere | Communication |
| Plants, Animals, Living things: Biosphere | Recreation |
| | Love |

# Ojibway Totem Animals and Qualities

| Animal | Quality | Animal | Quality |
|---|---|---|---|
| crane | leadership | hawk | foresight |
| eagle | courage, insight | seagull | grace, peace |
| loon | fidelity | black duck | depth |
| goose | prudence | sparrow hawk | perseverance |
| bear | strength, courage | moose | endurance, strength |
| marten | single-mindedness, judgment | wolf | perseverance, guardianship |
| lynx | determination | muskrat | endurance |
| beaver | resourcefulness, minding own business, | whitefish | abundance, fertility, beauty |
| sturgeon | depth, strength | pike | swiftness, elegance |
| merman | temptation | sucker | calmness, grace |
| mermaid | temptation | frog | transformation |
| water snake | willingness | catfish | breadth, scope |
| turtle | communication, messenger | rattlesnake | patience, slow to anger |

# Sound Suggestions for Developing Focus

Music that develops focus is even and regular with no unexpected changes that could be distracting. The tempo is generally moderate to slow. A continuous flow of pace and melody will allow continuous flow of thought. Classical music from the baroque era has a reliable pulse, rhythm, and harmonic progression that enhances focus. Collections of baroque music recordings have been designed specifically to maintain continuity and provide a uniform tempo. Baroque recordings of entire concertos that use both fast and slow movements, however, have also been found to be effective for enhancing focus. Certain Mozart selections from the classical era will work well for concentration, too.

Vocal music with recognizable words should not be used. Gregorian chant, with Latin words and long breathing patterns, can relax the body while allowing the mind to be alert. Piano music has a special ability to bring focus inward.

## Piano

Lanz, David Nightfall. *Return to the Heart*
Winston, George. *December, Autumn*

## Flute

Nakai, Carlos. *Cycles, Earth Spirit*
Rainer, John. *Songs of the Indian Flute*

## Gregorian chant

Hildegard of Bingen. *A Feather on the Breath of God*
Rutter, John. *Brother Sun, Sister Moon*
Utrecht Students' Chamber. *Officinum Tenebrarum*

## Slow Baroque Music

Short Selections

Albinoni, Tomaso. Adagio in G Minor for Strings and Organ
Bach, J. S. Air on a G String, "Jesu, Joy of Man's Desiring," "Sleeper's Awake"
Pachelbel, Johann. Canon in D

Collections

Celestial Harmonies. *Adagio I* or *Adagio II*
LIND Institute. *Relax with the Classics*, Nos. 1–4 (Andante, Adagio, Pastorale, Largo)

## Baroque Selections with a Variety of Tempos

Bach, J. S. *Brandenburg Concertos*, especially no. 2
Barzak Educational Institute. *Baroque Music No. 1* or *Baroque Music No. 2*
Campbell, Don. *Cosmic Classics* (side 1)

Concertos or sonatas by Johann Sebastian Bach, Arcangelo Corelli,
George Frederick Handel, Pietro Locatelli, Georg Phillip Telemann,
or Antonio Vivaldi

Handel, George Frederick. *Water Music, Royal Fireworks Suite*
Rutter, John. *The Handel Collection*
Vivaldi, Antonio. *The Four Seasons*

## Most recordings of the following Mozart selections

C Major Piano Concerto
Any of the Mozart divertimentos
*Eine Kleine Nachtmusik*
Prague and Haffner Symphonies
Rutter, John (conductor). *The Mozart Collection*

# Sound Suggestions for Relaxation

The music that helps people concentrate will often work well as relaxation
music. Certain music will move the listener even more deeply into a relaxation
state, however. This music is often slower than the concentration selections.
Consistency is important. A repeated slow pulsation will entrain the listener to
a relaxed pace. A different but also effective style for relaxation creates a free-
flow feeling without any discernible pulse. Harp, flute, electronic sounds, and
string ensembles are very effective instruments for relaxation music.

Aeoliah. *Angel Love*
Campbell, Don. *Angels* (side 2), *Crystal Meditations, Runes*
  (for deep relaxation)
Chacra Artists. *New Age of Classics: Bach* (with ocean sounds)
Halpern, Steven. *Spectrum Suite, Dawn*
Horn, Paul. *The Peace Album*
Kobialka, Daniel. *Velvet Dreams* (string music)
Robertson, Kim. *Wind Shadows,* vols. 1 and 2 (Celtic harp)
Sill, Gary. *Pachelbel with Ocean*

# Sound Suggestions for Movement and Energy

For movement activities, music with a steady rhythm will help students feel
comfortable in moving, will set a rhythm, and will keep energy levels high.
Music with a high energy flow is just as effective as music with a constant heavy
beat. Music with words will be just as effective as instrumental music. Some-
times the addition of lyrics is beneficial if the words are appropriate for the
classroom.

Listen to a music selection before using it in class to make sure it will be appropriate for your activity.

Brubeck, Dave. "Take Five"
Joplin, Scott. Ragtime music
Lewis, Brent. *Earth Tribe Rhythms*
Louis Clark, Royal Philharmonic Orchestra. *Hooked on Classics*
Lynch, Ray. *Deep Breakfast*
Mannheim Steamroller. *Saving the Wildlife,* "Wolfgang Amadeus Penguin"
Rowland, Mike. *Fairy Ring*
Sousa, John Phillip. Marches
Strauss, Johann. Waltzes
Synchestra. *Mother Earth's Lullaby*
Tchaikovsky, Peter Illyich. Waltzes
Winter, Paul. *Earthbeat*
Yanni. *Keys to Imagination*

Experiment with lively Motown songs, 1950s rock n' roll, Celtic Irish music, disco or break-dance music, jazz, or exciting movie soundtracks.

# Sound Suggestions for Imagery

Music for imagery has diverse characteristics depending on its use. To provide background sound during a guided imagery, find music that is simple, flowing, and harmonious. You will need to choose long selections to avoid distracting breaks between cuts. If music is used as a stimulus for imagery but not as background sound for a guided visualization, music that is expressive, interesting, and variable will stimulate a greater variety of imagery.

## Guided Visualization Background Music

Bearns and Dexter. *Golden Voyage,* vols. 1–4
Halpern, Steven. *Soundwave 2000 Series: Creativity, Spectrum Suite*
Kobialka, Daniel. *Velvet Dreams*
Rowland, Mike. *Fairy Ring*
Sill, Gary. *Pachelbel with Ocean*

## Music to Stimulate Imagery

Debussy, Claude. *La Mer*
Gardner, Kay. *Rainbow Path*
Holst, Gustav. *The Planets*
Kitaro. *Silk Road Suite*
Mannheim Steamroller. *Saving the Wildlife*
Shardad. *Beauty of Love*
Sill, Gary. *Pachelbel with Ocean*
Winter, Paul. *Earthbeat, Wolf Eyes*

# Sound Suggestions for Inspiration

Sound connections are made through inspirational lyrics or sheer power of sound. The following songs can be used to make sound connections for self-worth, cooperation, inspiration, and caring. Don't forget to ask students to bring in songs that they find inspirational and moving.

Armstrong, Louis. "What a Wonderful World"
Cara, Irene. "What a Feeling" (from *Flashdance*)
Collins, Judy. "Both Sides Now"
Denver, John. "I Want to Live"
Diamond, Neil. "He Ain't Heavy"
Flack, Roberta. "Reach Out and Touch Someone"
Franklin, Aretha. "Look to the Rainbow"
Houston, Whitney. "One Moment in Time," "Greatest Love of All"
Ingram, James, and Linda Ronstadt. "Somewhere Out There"
Jackson, Michael. "The Man in the Mirror," "It's as Easy as 1, 2, 3"
King, B. B. "Stand by Me"
King, Carole. "You've Got a Friend"
McFerrin, Bobby. "Don't Worry, Be Happy"
Any recording of "Man from La Mancha" (The Impossible Dream)
Midler, Bette. "From a Distance," "Wind beneath My Wings"
Pomeranz, David. "It's in Every One of Us"
Quist, Rob. "Back in Harmony"
Simon, Carly. "Let the River Run"
Simon, Paul, and Garfunkel, Art. "Bridge over Troubled Waters"
Sonny and Cher. "The Beat of a Different Drummer"
South, Joe. "Walk a Mile in My Shoes"

The following albums have a number of appropriate songs on them:

Denver, John. *Seasons of the Heart*
Grammer, Red. *Teaching Peace*
Jackson, Michael. *Heal the World*
Lasar, Mars. *Olympus* (instrumental)
Lynch, Ray. *Deep Breakfast* (instrumental)
*The 1988 Summer Olympics,* especially "One Moment in Time"
Tesh, John. *The Games* (instrumental music from sports games)

# Aha!!

By Chris Brewer, with Jean Houston

Chorus:
The answer is there for all to see.
It lies inside of you and me
And when we hear what it has to say
We see the start of a brand new day!
Aha! Aha! Aha! Aha!

But let's get back to reality.
It's not my problem, don't you see?
And when it comes 'round to me
I don't have authority.
We're too busy for that.
People will laugh.
It will probably fall flat!
We've always done it this way before,
But we can't seem to get our foot in the door.
Oh how hard do we fight
To keep old patterns in our sight!

*(Chorus)*

The new idea that you submit—
Just send it out in triplicate.
It's kicked upstairs to you know who.
The word comes down—Catch 22!!
Subsection 1, Paragraph 3,
Item 9, Addendum B.
See above and what do you know—
It says up there to see below!

*(Chorus)*

Creativity can open the door
And soon you'll find more and more.
So when you need to make a change
You'll find a way to rearrange.
You can whistle a tune
Or doodle till noon.
Oh you'll find a way
To make work play

*(Chorus)*

Make the time to incubate.
You'll find the answers are first rate.
You can make the problems blow away
If creativity has its say.
Believe in yourself and your insight.
There's lots of ways to make things right.
You're as creative as you feel.
It's as easy as that . . . what a deal!

*(Chorus)*

Aha! Aha! Aha! Aha!

Note: Verses 4 and 5 are by Jean Houston, adapted from
"SYS-TEM" (Brewer and Campbell [1991]).

# Bibliography

Bean, Reynold, and Harris Clemes. *Self-Esteem: The Key to Your Child's Well-Being.* New York: Putnam, 1981.

Beane, James A., and Richard P. Lipka. *Self-Concept, Self-Esteem, and the Curriculum.* New York: Teachers College Press, 1984.

Benzwie, Teresa. *A Moving Experience: Dance for Lovers of Children and the Child Within.* Tucson, Ariz.: Zephyr Press, 1988.

Borba, Michele. *Esteem Builders: A Self-Esteem Curriculum for Improving Student Achievement, Behavior, and School/Home Climate.* Rolling Hills Estates, Calif.: Jalmar Press, 1989.

Borba, Michele, and Craig Borba. *Self-Esteem—A Classroom Affair: 101 Ways to Help Children Like Themselves.* Vol. 2. Rolling Hills Estates, Calif.: Jalmar Press, 1982.

Branden, Nathaniel. *The Psychology of Self-Esteem.* New York: Bantam, 1969.

Brewer, Chris. "Rhythms of Education." *Open Ear.* Winter 1992.

Brewer, Chris, and Don G. Campbell. *Rhythms of Learning: Creative Tools for Developing Lifelong Skills.* Tucson, Ariz.: Zephyr Press, 1991.

Briggs, Dorothy. *Your Child's Self-Esteem: The Key to His Life.* Garden City, N.Y.: Doubleday, 1970.

California Task Force to Promote Self-Esteem and Personal and Social Responsibility. *Toward a State of Esteem.* Sacramento, Calif.: California State Department of Education, 1990.

Campbell, Robert W. *The New Science—Self-Esteem Psychology.* Lanham, Md.: University Press of America, 1984.

Canfield, Jack, and H. Wells. *100 Ways to Enhance Self-Concept in the Classroom: A Handbook for Teachers and Parents.* Englewood Cliffs, N.J.: Prentice Hall, 1976.

Clark, Aminah, Harris Clemes, and Reynold Bean. *How to Raise Teenager Self-Esteem.* San Jose, Calif.: Enrich, 1983.

Clark, Jean Illsley. *Self-Esteem: The Key to Your Child's Well-Being.* New York: G. P. Putnam's Sons, 1981.

Coopersmith, Stanley. *The Antecedents of Self-Esteem.* San Francisco: W. H. Freeman, 1967.

Damon, William, and Daniel Hart. *Self-Understanding in Childhood and Adolescents.* New York: Cambridge University Press, 1988.

de Bono, Edward. *Six Thinking Hats.* Boston: Little, Brown, 1985.

———, *Six Action Shoes.* New York: HarperCollins, HarperBusiness, 1991.

Dennison, Paul E., and Gail E. Dennison. *Brain Gym: Simple Activities for Whole Brain Learning.* Ventura, Calif.: Edu-Kinesthetics, 1986.

Drew, Naomi. *Learning the Skills of Peacemaking: Communicating, Cooperation, Resolving Conflict.* Creative Teaching Series. Rolling Hills Estates, Calif.: Jalmar Press, 1987.

Felker, Donald W. *Building Positive Self-Concepts.* Minneapolis, Minn.: Burgess Publishing, 1974.

Fox, C. Lynn, and Francine L. Weaver. *Unlocking Doors to Self-Esteem.* Rolling Hills Estates, Calif.: Jalmar Press, 1990.

Fugitt, Eva D. *He Hit Me Back First: Self-Esteem through Self-Discipline.* Rolling Hills Estates, Calif.: Jalmar Press, 1983.

Gang, Philip S. *Our Planet, Our Home: A Global Vision of Ecology.* Tucson, Ariz.: Zephyr Press, 1992.

Gilbert, Anne Green. *Teaching the Three R's through Movement Experiences: A Handbook for Teachers.* New York: Macmillan, 1977.

Goode, Caron B., and Joy Lehni Watson. *The Mind Fitness Program for Esteem and Excellence: Guided Stories for Imagery in Whole-Brain Learning.* Tucson, Ariz.: Zephyr Press, 1992.

————. *Reaching the Star Within.* Audiotape to accompany *The Mind Fitness Program for Esteem and Excellence.* Tucson, Ariz.: Zephyr Press, 1992.

Greene, Brad, and Shayle Uroff. *Self-Esteem—A Manual for Helping Others.* Simi Valley, Calif.: 4 A's Associates, 1989.

Gurney, Peter. *Self-Esteem in Children with Special Needs.* New York: Routledge, 1988.

Harmin, Merril. *Spunjz: Langage Arts ACtivities for Self-Awareness.* Tucson, Ariz.: Zephyr Press, 1992.

Hartline, Jo Ellen. *Me!? A Curriculum for Teaching Self-Esteem through an Interest Center.* Rev. ed. Tucson, Ariz.: Zephyr Press, 1990.

Henley, Thom. *Rediscovery: Ancient Pathways—New Directions.* Vancouver: Western Canada Wilderness Committee, 1989.

Kehayan, V. Alex. *Self-Awareness Growth Experiences.* Creative Teaching Series. Rolling Hills Estates, Calif.: Jalmar Press, 1989.

Klare, Judy. *Looking Good—Self-Esteem.* Vero Beach, Fla.: Vero Publications, 1989.

Lalli, Judy. *Feelings Alphabet: An Album of Emotions from A to Z.* Rolling Hills Estates, California: B. L. Winch, 1984.

Lipka, R. P., and T. M. Brinthapt, eds. *Studying the Self: Perspective across Life-Span.* New York: Teachers College Press, 1990.

McDaniel, Sandy, and Peggy Bielen. *Project Self-Esteem.* Rev. ed. Creative Teaching Series. Rolling Hills Estates, Calif.: Jalmar Press, 1990.

Margulies, Nancy. *Mapping Inner Space: Learning and Teaching Mind Mapping.* Tucson, Ariz: Zephyr Press, 1991.

Marston, Stephanie. *The Magic of Encouragement: Nurturing Your Child's Self-Esteem.* William Morrow, 1990.

Mecca, Andrew, Neil J. Smelser, and John Vasconcellos, eds. *The Social Importance of Self-Esteem.* Berkeley, California: The University of California Press, 1989.

Naisbitt, John, and Patricia Aburdene. *Megatrends 2000.* New York: William Morrow, 1990.

Pendergast, Susan, and Jayne Devencenzi. *Belonging—A Guide for Group Facilitators: Self and Social Discovery for Children of All Ages.* Reprint. San Luis Obispo, Calif.: Belonging, 1988.

Purkey, William W. *Self-Concept and School Achievement.* Englewood Cliffs, N.J.: Prentice Hall, 1970.

———. *Inviting School Success: A Self-Concept Approach to Teaching and Learning.* Belmont, Calif.: Wadsworth Publishing, 1978.

Reps, Paul. "Pillow Education in Rural Japan." In *Square Sun, Square Moon.* New York: Tuttle, 1967.

Salmon, Linda Suzanne. *Applause! Activities for Building Confidence through Dramatic Arts.* Tucson, Ariz.: Zephyr Press, 1992.

Satir, Virginia. *Self-Esteem.* Millbrae, Calif.: Celestial Arts, 1975.

Simon, Sidney. *Caring, Feeling, Touching.* Niles, Ill.: Argus Communications, 1976.

Steinem, Gloria. *Revolution from Within: A Book of Self-Esteem.* Boston, Mass.: Little, Brown, 1992.

Stoddard, Lynn. *Redesigning Education: A Guide for Developing Human Greatness.* Tucson, Ariz.: Zephyr Press, 1992.

Wade, Rahima Carol. *Joining Hands.* Tucson, Ariz.: Zephyr Press, 1991.

# NOTES

# NOTES

# NOTES

# Additional Resources from Zephyr Press

## ME!?
### A Curriculum for Teaching Self-Esteem through an Interest Center
by Jo Ellen Hartline

This book is chock-full of ways to enhance self-esteem in your students every day. A noted teacher and workshop presenter in self-esteem, Jo Ellen Hartline brings together myriad resources for setting up a Self-Esteem Learning Center.

You'll have the inspiration you need to bring out the best in your students. Plus, you'll have activities, awards, bulletin board ideas, poems, lists of recommended books and films, and background material.

This revised edition saves you time with its easy organization.You'll have simple yet effective methods for helping your students learn to appreciate their individuality.

Grades K–8.
152 pages, 8 1/2" x 11", softbound.
ZB04-W . . . $21


## LIFE CYCLE
### Classroom Activities for Helping Children Live with Daily Change and Loss
by Jeanne Lagorio, M.S.W.

Children are increasingly forced to confront losses early in life. With the sensitive activities in *Life Cycle*, you can help your students understand and handle these changes effectively, as well as build those skills necessary to cope with losses in the future.

*Life Cycle* provides seven activities for K–1 and seven sessions of activities each for 2– and 5–6. Each K–1 activity and each session runs about 50 minutes and is easily adaptable for individual, small-group, and classroom settings.

Grades K–6.
128 pages, 7" x 10" softbound.
ZB36-W . . . $19.95

## REDESIGNING EDUCATION
### A Guide for Developing Human Greatness
by Lynn Stoddard

Here's a framework you can use to restructure your educational environment to help children develop three dimensions of greatness—their individual talents, their powers of communication, and their creative minds.

This new framework contains eight components—
1. **The Mission of Education**—to develop people who are valuable contributors to society
2. **Master Goals**—the three dimensions of human greatness: identity, interaction, and inquiry
3. **Equal Partnerships**—with teachers and parents working together
4. **A Take-Charge Philosophy**—with curriculum as a means not an end
5. **Evaluation of Greatness**—to assess student growth for feedback and guidance
6. **Multiple Intelligences**—acknowledging that each child has a unique set     of gifts
7. **How the Brain Works**—recognizing that we learn through self-initiated inquiry
8. **Strategies for Greatness**—how-to steps that emerge as students hold visions of their own greatness

For teachers of K–Adult.
104 pages, 7" x 9", softbound.
ZB27-W . . . $19


## HOW TO BECOME AN EXPERT
### Discover, Research, and Build a Project in Your Chosen Field
by Maurice Gibbons

Guide your students through the stages of becoming an expert in areas that they define. They start by becoming explorers  then specialists . . . then apprentices who create products related to their areas of expertise.

Your students will learn to empower themselves to set their own goals, make plans for reaching those goals, and then follow through with their plans to the best of their abilities. They'll get lots of encouragement—and even a few laughs!

Grades 5–8.
136 pages, 8 1/2" x 11", softbound.
ZB16-W . . . $19.95

*To order, write or call—*

Zephyr Press
P.O. Box 66006-W
Tucson, Arizona 85728-6006
Phone—(602) 322-5090
FAX—(602) 323-9402

You can also request a free copy of our current catalog showing other learning materials that foster whole-brain learning, creative thinking, and self-awareness.

**Zephyr** Press

REACHING THEIR HIGHEST POTENTIAL